Beyond Welcome

Building Communities of Love

Edited by Linnea Nelson

Skinner House Books
Boston

skinnerhouse.org

Printed in the United States

Text and cover design by Tim Holtz
Author photo by Joel Nelson

print ISBN: 978-1-55896-882-0
eBook ISBN: 978-1-55896-883-7

5 4 3 2 1
25 24 23 22 21

Library of Congress Cataloging-in-Publication Data
Names: Nelson, Linnea, editor.
Title: Beyond welcome : building communities of love / edited by Linnea Nelson.
Description: Boston : Skinner House Books, [2021] | Summary: "In Beyond Welcome: Building Communities of Love, editor Linnea Nelson and contributors dream of a future Unitarian Universalism that upholds abundant love and universal justice within every community. The lived experiences of these hopeful Unitarian Universalists-ministers, religious professionals, and laypeople alike-illuminate the relevancy of liberation in each and every one of our communities. Examining both the joys of community and the responsibilities we have to one another, Beyond Welcome provides clarity about current structures and behaviors that create barriers to equity in our faith communities as a passageway to building foundational structures of love and liberation"-- Provided by publisher.
Identifiers: LCCN 2021046389 (print) | LCCN 2021046390 (ebook) | ISBN 9781558968820 (print) | ISBN 9781558968837 (ebook)
Subjects: LCSH: Unitarian Universalist churches. | Love--Religious aspects--Unitarian Universalist churches. | Communities--Religious aspects--Unitarian Universalist churches.
Classification: LCC BX9855 .B49 2021 (print) | LCC BX9855 (ebook) | DDC 230.07/391--dc23
LC record available at https://lccn.loc.gov/2021046389
LC ebook record available at https://lccn.loc.gov/2021046390

Contents

Once more we form the circle
Shoulder to shoulder
Against the cold night
Breaths rising
Flames passing
Candle to candle

Hands sheltering the tender light
Against the night wind
Eyes reflecting flame
Voices lifting "Silent Night"

And when my light blows out
Again
You offer yours

—Kristen Moyer, "Under the Night Sky"

Introduction

The experiences and perspectives you will read in this book deliver vital truths in Unitarian Universalism. *Beyond Welcome: Building Communities of Love* explores liberation through personal and collective reflections on belonging. These heartfelt essays explore the essence of what it means to each author to be in Unitarian Universalist community. They provide clarity about our current structures and behaviors and a way forward in love and justice. The lived experiences of these hopeful Unitarian Universalists illuminate how the work of liberation is relevant in every one of our faith communities. Through story and example, readers of this book, especially groups who read it together, will find more ways to live into the essence of Unitarian Universalism.

With each essay, it becomes clearer that our work is not done. If we cultivate a Buddhist beginner's mind and recognize that we are always just beginning, we can fully appreciate and honor our faith's past dedication to civil rights, our Welcoming Congregation program, and the other ways Unitarian Universalists have created a more inclusive world, while still recognizing that our work is ongoing.

Our recent experiences with a global pandemic, political turmoil, and the increasing visibility of ongoing and violent cultures of oppression compound our yearning for Beloved Community. The experiences recounted in this book are varied and personal. Each essay begins with a question that invites personal consideration, such as "What are my own experiences in community?" Before you read the essay, take a few moments to reflect deeply on the question. Discover whether you are tapping into abundance or scarcity, love or fear. And each essay also ends with a question, this time one that invites a collective response, such as "How does my congregation or organization need to change culture or structures in order to allow everyone to fully engage and belong?" Reflect on and respond to this question with a partner or a group. If you serve on a board or committee that is reading the book together, take time in each meeting to reflect on one of the essays, to learn from the essayist and one another, and to add to your collective wisdom. These conversations will spur the building of fair and equitable congregational systems and reimagine power structures to create authentic relationships. They will open your hearts to the shared liberation that creates true belonging.

These essays were written just before and during the COVID-19 pandemic, during which we were experiencing the additional challenge of learning how to create community while physically distanced. Even as we struggle to remain connected online, we are being challenged to go beyond merely welcoming people. By taking a closer look at both the joys of belonging and the responsibilities we have to one another, we can use this time to develop a spiritual power that will sustain us in the work of justice.

We have so much to learn about being together. Elandria Williams, former co-moderator of the UUA, upholds the relevance of this work and helps us recognize that it is just beginning: "We're actually going to put all our organizing at work in how we build community, how we build spaces of restoration, how we actually help each other realize we are worthy enough to be restored and well. . . . You can't have abolition if you don't have free space. And if we're not liberated as individuals and as people and as community, we're not gonna be liberated. Period. Cuz we don't know what that feels like."

As we begin again to learn how to create communities of collective love and influence, we will be transforming the remnants of historically power-centric policies. Dr. Mark Hicks notes that "congregations want to 'close the gap' between their aspirations and the challenging reality of actually becoming multiracial, multicultural, theologically and generationally diverse spiritual communities." We can do this by going "beyond welcome" as a faith community, to work shoulder to shoulder as we create foundational structures to live into liberation.

We need to ask ourselves, "Who is asking to be a part of our Beloved Communities? What is holding them apart?" These essays will call you and your community to focus on the barriers and equity issues in your own faith community and to honestly wrestle with these questions. I hope they prompt you to discuss how to make worship more accessible to more people, how to build leadership teams that represent the community you aspire to be, and how you will listen more deeply to one another in order to support and engage the entire community. We will learn new ways of being together that live out the dreams of Unitarian Universalism.

This work is impossible to do alone. So I highly recommend that committees, boards, teams, and small group ministries read and reflect on these essays together. All of us must learn from one another to see more clearly the structures that too often remain invisible to the individual. Together we can free ourselves from the burdens we have inherited. Everyday structures that are often invisible to those in power can be reimagined to create more positive environments that foster our collective strength.

These essays are gifts from their authors. It is rare that any one of us can hear directly and personally from so many people who are willing to share their experiences so intimately. I acknowledge that no single voice represents any group of people, any single identity, or even any specific intersection of identities. Each writer is reflecting on their own experience and binding it to hope for our future. May these voices lift us to appreciate the intersection of our identities and experiences to form more loving, compassionate, authentic, and equitable communities.

Linnea Nelson, April 2021

Built Through Trust

Rev. Manish Mishra-Marzetti

What are the requirements of membership in the places you belong?

Belonging as elitism

"Membership has its privileges," the slogan of the 1980s American Express ad campaign, concisely captures the way that belonging can define who has access to something elite and worthy of holding onto and who does not. When we notice that belonging is often delicately intertwined with power, privilege, access, status, and resources, we begin to see how it can become a form of social currency that can be owned and bestowed. If doing so benefits me, I can make you feel special, make you feel that you belong, and if doing so becomes inconvenient, if it does not meet my needs, I can withdraw my acknowledgment that you belong. Who belongs and who does not belong becomes a tool in the mediation of control, power, and resources: an extension of capitalist and colonialist domination-oriented thinking. New and "different" individuals are treated with distrust; they must prove their worth and earn their place.

This worldview deeply informs certain approaches to belonging. In our Unitarian Universalist circles, we might encounter, at times, questions related to the financial sustainability of a community. Invariably, at that juncture, outreach strategies and newcomers are invoked. Whether it is directly articulated or not, the premise behind these comments is that we need new people in the community because we need their money. Offering others a sense of belonging becomes a financial strategy. Or, perhaps, the same cadre of congregational leaders is tired from having led the same programs and activities for so long. Here too, invariably, the conversation turns to newer people in the community: how do we get new people to lead the activities and programs that have been beloved, in the same way that the familiar leaders have? In both of these scenarios, newer members are framed, explicitly or implicitly, as a commodity—a commodity that has utility for those who already belong. In his conceptualization of the "categorial imperative," the philosopher Immanuel Kant spoke vociferously against treating other human beings as a means to an end. We are not actually honoring the humanity of others when we do so; we are treating them like an "it," an object of benefit to us.

Part of our work, as a people committed to the inherent dignity and worth of all, is to examine and confront implicit and explicit human constructs that lift up some people as more worthy than others. Our natural desire to honor our individual uniqueness and personal gifts need not come at the cost of placing others beneath us or treating others as a means to an end. There is a better way.

Belonging as an unconditional facet of existence

In 2010, I attended a traditional Shoshone gathering, knowing only one or two people there. I was a total newcomer, and yet

I found myself embraced and greeted warmly, with smiles, by virtually everyone I encountered. Meals were shared. Songs and teachings were shared. I was offered opportunities to speak and share my journey with others. I was given gifts by people who I have never seen since then. Feeling so profoundly included and welcomed in this way was both beautiful and staggering. No one was expecting anything from me in return for the warmth I was greeted with. I was treated as if I fully belonged because, in this spiritual-theological worldview, I did. I belonged because I showed up, because I chose to be in community with others.

What I encountered in this particular circle was what I have consistently encountered in Indigenous wisdom traditions around the world: belonging is not a commodity, a form of social currency, that is owned or hoarded; it is not something that I must wrest from the world or others around me. Belonging, in this very different framework, is implicitly woven into the fabric of all that exists. There is nothing on our planet that does not belong, and all that exists is finely interconnected and interrelated. Would I tell the first spring robin that it doesn't belong on my lawn? Would I tell an earthworm that the ground it lives in belongs to me and not to it? Of course not. In this worldview, we belong, and others belong to us, because we coexist: we share space, we share our lives, we share the nature-given resources of this world with one another.

Intertwined coexistence, rather than elitism, can provide a very different grounding for our sense of belonging. Elitism invites us to bolster our own self-esteem by controlling and limiting who belongs. In contrast, honoring our coexistence, together in community, invites me to unconditionally honor your worthiness because you are here, in community with me; because you are navigating fundamental human needs and concerns, the same as me. I, then, have to trust that you will reciprocate and honor my humanity and dignity in a similar way. Belonging, in this worldview, rests in, and is defined by, a sense of mutuality.

Embodied communities of practice

Mutual regard, concern, and trust have no meaning as purely intellectual constructs. They must be embodied and brought alive through our words and deeds. Because of this, I often refer to Unitarian Universalist communities as "communities of practice." Framed by rigorous thought and defined by our commitment to love, community is the place where we practice bringing alive our most cherished values. Without that embodiment, the values we espouse are merely theoretical.

We live into our values in a given time, a given moment in history that links past and future through the present. From that place of historicity, Unitarian Universalism is undeniably a tradition that has sought to appeal to the widest swath of humanity possible, via our noncreedal, personal growth-oriented, and justice-focused approach to spirituality. We have, to some degree, been successful in precisely that mission that our humanistic forebears envisioned; we have found expressions of religion that have, indeed, over time, transcended any one culture, art form, theology, music, race, ethnicity, or other identity markers. In this success lie our deepest contemporary challenges and opportunities.

As our tradition has, over time, progressively grown broader and more diverse, we have tended to hold tightly to established

expressions of religiosity—the cultural expressions of Unitarian Universalism, as reflected in our music, art, language, etc.
We are simultaneously living into the 1920-30s humanistic
vision of being a broad-based, far-reaching spiritual movement, and at the same time expecting that those who join us
will conform to the styles of art, music, language, and other
forms of expression that have preceded. We Unitarian Universalists can thus wind up holding dogmatic cultural expectations, despite our intentionally noncreedal, broad-based
tradition. The newcomer is often sent the subtle message, "If
you like what we have typically sung, read, talked about, and
admired, then you probably belong. Just be sure to learn our
cultural norms, because we are not going to learn yours, even
if we all agree on the UU Principles and Sources." Cultural
norms can, in this manner, silently become a Unitarian Universalist vetting process upon which belonging is conditioned.

But this is not true across Unitarian Universalism. The
opposite of centering one, or primarily one, cultural expression of Unitarian Universalism is intentionally sharing the
center with a variety of cultural forms and expressions. What
is highlighted, what is visited—theologically, musically, artis-
tically, linguistically—over time moves toward a multiplicity
of expression. We can rotate the thinkers, systems of thought,
and theological paradigms we refer to. We can, accountably
and in relationship, draw on innumerable artistic and musical
forms that capture Unitarian Universalist values.

Trusting the people, all of the people

We often wind up thinking and believing that we need to
look outside our local community to find varied cultural

expressions of Unitarian Universalism. But the Unitarian Universalists who are already among us hold a variety of cultural expressions of our faith; we simply have not yet learned how to draw more deeply and relationally on them. Thinking of diversity as something that exists outside of Unitarian Universalism keeps us from understanding that the work of building a broader and deeper sense of belonging is not externally oriented: we Unitarian Universalists are already—today—the most diverse we have ever been, and yet our forms and ways of expressing ourselves are not.

Do we, as Unitarian Universalists, trust those who relate to Unitarian Universalism differently from the way we personally might? If we cannot find our way to that sense of mutuality—mutual trust, mutual understanding, and mutual commitment to our faith—we are doomed to war. For not trusting our siblings in faith is to pit ourselves against them; it is to believe that if the "other" truly belongs, then I "lose" something—perhaps prominence, perhaps control, perhaps what has been familiar.

The Indigenous cultures in which I have experienced mutuality are not fear- or control-oriented. There is no fear that those who arrive will somehow change everything. Rather, it is understood that all will adjust to create the sense of community that is needed right now; therefore, all belong. There is an intentional and nurtured generosity of spirit in this. What has previously been is honored and valued, for how could it not be? The present does not emerge from a vacuum. The future, in turn, takes shape in relationship to all that has been, intersecting with the people and the needs that we are present to now. Continuity exists, and within that continuity exist relationships, ancestors, sacrifices, values, dreams, visions, and a shared journey into the future.

adrienne maree brown invites us to "trust the people" (adriennemareebrown.net/2019/07/01/trust-the-people-2). Not "some of the people," or "the people we like best," but *the* people: all of the people. For Unitarian Universalists, this serves as a call to honor and include all who have sincerely chosen to journey with us. It requires a grounding in mutuality and multiplicity, one that can hold, and meaningfully speak to, the breadth and depth of who we already are, as a movement, today. This is doable. We just need to set aside our fear and choose community—over and over again.

What fears might be lurking behind resistance to change in your community?

Covenant and Community

Julica Hermann de la Fuente and Christina Rivera

What value do we place on a shared covenant?

Covenanting and how we use covenants are among the most important factors in determining whether our faith communities will maintain the status quo by running away from conflict or liberate us to challenge white supremacy culture by dealing with conflict in productive ways. Covenants embody how we're going to be with each other as we move forward.

Individualism is connected to white supremacy culture and also shows up in many covenants. A covenant created to protect oneself is very different from the covenant that emerges from a commitment to make the community stronger —to make everyone involved safe. Particularly in Unitarian Universalist spaces, a covenant is often a promise to bring all that we are and speak our truth. But if the covenant assumes an equal power dynamic among everyone involved, it might not provide any safety for people with more marginalized identities. A good covenant needs to serve the needs of people with diverse social locations and access to power. We must remember that people with different identities must all feel safe in order to commit to a covenant.

We're not all being asked to do the same thing. In a multi-racial group of ministers where the white folks said, "We want to take risks!" a colleague of color responded, "That's great for you. I want to protect myself more. I'm risking all the time. I need the opposite of risk taking." We need to understand the levels of risk people are able to tolerate while we are living into a bold space. Some people can risk having their feelings hurt, but they can't risk having their body hurt. Someone in a different social location may be able to risk physical injury, because any harm they do suffer is less likely to be severe. To give another example, a racialized immigrant may not feel able to risk being arrested, even if they are a citizen, because their safety in that situation is more tenuous than that of a white citizen would be. A good covenant acknowledges that *safety* and *risk* mean different things to different people.

Covenants are often used to protect and respond to white fragility. Often covenants include a phrase like "We assume good intentions." But people of color may wonder, "Do we? I don't assume good intentions." "We intend well" too often means "If I hurt your feelings, it's not my fault, because I had good intentions." The more powerful way of engaging this work is to say, "I'll be more responsible for my impact and worry later about my intentions." Impact is the place where we're going to focus, not whether we intended hurt or not.

Note that people who live with disabilities ask us not to use the word *brave*. *Brave* can be a trigger word, since the disabled are often told how brave they are just for living. If your community has shifted its covenanting language from "safe spaces" to "brave spaces," discuss shifting further to speak of "bold spaces."

We also need to make room for the emotional work of messing up. A good covenant makes room for feelings but also has processes for how to engage the feelings when they show up so that the group's process isn't hijacked or arrested by one person having difficulty.

In good covenants, we focus on power dynamics, risk taking, social location, and impact over intent, but congregations too often leave out making space for the holy, especially when they have difficulty with religious language. Since people experience the holy in different ways, crafting covenants and living into covenants can actually bring us closer to the holy. When we're doing soulful and faithful covenantal work, bringing somebody back into covenant, it opens our hearts to the holy. Just being able to acknowledge that one is feeling the spiritual or holy in the moment, with the other people in the covenanting process, has value that can't be quantified. Just starting to name these moments would get us closer to our Unitarian Universalist theology, which calls us to build a heaven on earth in which everyone is saved. What an exciting theology! Instead of worrying, "Oh no, we're going to start talking about religion. Are we all going to be okay?" we can just say, "This is sacred," and doing that makes it so.

When people can experience covenanting that is not damaging, that does not presuppose any particular belief or belief system, they are able to say, "Wow, yeah, that was an okay experience. Somebody just named something that I hadn't thought about before. And the world didn't come to a screeching halt. It actually felt kind of good. I'm going to think about that the next time I'm looking for a way through something."

In Unitarian Universalist contexts we often start with the covenant, to make sure everybody knows the rules before we start doing the work together. Instead, step back and get to know each other just a little bit first. Tell about your dog or your kids; break bread together; share what kind of music you like to listen to. Having even a small amount of human connection with one another before we try to figure out how we're going to be with each other is a way to build the trust needed for a covenant.

Covenanting often goes better when we focus on feelings more than on wordsmithing and precision. To begin a covenant, invite people to remember a time when they were in a group that was functioning really well. Ask them to go back to that time and remember it as sensorially as possible: *How did it smell? How did it look? How did it sound? How did it feel? Where were you? What was the temperature in the room? How did people treat each other? How did you feel? How did you and others behave? What behaviors were absent?* Take the time to name all the things remembered. Ask them to write the feelings and behaviors on sticky notes. Then put the sticky notes on a wall and group them. What's amazing is that people doing this exercise write the same things over and over and over again. *Love, trust, respect, patience, truth-telling* — all of these ways of being together are important to us. Once the notes are on the wall and everyone has had a chance to name several things, less discussion is needed, because people feel heard and they feel included. And then you can usually say easily, "So, do we have agreement? Obviously, we already do!"

Do a gallery walk to read through the notes. Take a moment to take them in. Then ask, "Can we agree that we already know how to do this because we've already been in those spaces? And can we just trust that we can bring our best selves to this space?" Folks are so surprised when they realize that they have already created their covenant.

The covenanting process should take into account the amount of time the covenanting body will be together. When the group will persist over a long period—as a committee or task force is likely to, for instance—you'll need to ask more specific questions, such as "What will we do when conflict arises?" You may not need to bring such questions to a one-time workshop, because it isn't necessary to belabor the point, but remind everyone that they already have the skills.

Sometimes people joining an existing group will say, "Well, I didn't come up with that covenant. I didn't agree. I wasn't part of the drafting process. How can you hold me accountable to something that I had no say in?" Do you want to create a new covenant each time someone new arrives? Yes and no. You don't want to take all the time that it takes to start from scratch. But you do need to give all participants the opportunity to say, "Okay, I agree." Congregations might offer a membership class that explains to potential members that joining the congregation means agreeing to certain ways of being. A board that is welcoming new members may want to deconstruct its covenant a little more and rebuild it so that all its members feel ownership of it, because the board is going to do hard, intense work together and needs mutual support.

Our colleague Andrée Mol says, "We're really good at creating covenant, but we don't live into it really well." Keeping a covenant visible helps groups cope when something goes wrong. Being able to point to a clause of the covenant and say, "I think there's something in here that's happening right now. Can we talk about it?" can help keep things from getting out of hand. Youth groups are often much better at this than adults. Youth tend to be particularly good at saying, "Okay, yeah, let's talk about that," without defensiveness, fear that someone's going to get in trouble, or shaming anyone, and in this they set a good example for the rest of us. When reminded of their covenant, youth often acknowledge that they committed to being a certain way with each other and may not be living up to that commitment in the moment. For some reason, that ability to move back and reflect is too often lost in adulthood. In adult spaces, people tend to get defensive, and it can be much harder to call adults back into covenant.

When facilitating a group, you can use the covenant as a source of your power and authority. For example, if a comment is out of covenant, you can invoke the group's covenant and your role as its keeper to ask the group to refrain from such comments. It's helpful to have allies in the room who can also name what's happening and affirm the same understanding of the covenant.

You might ask members of the group to show up with their best self. Then participate and lead from a place of vulnerability and authenticity, centering feelings, which will invite participants to do the same. If a facilitator shows up as an expert and gets defensive, people respond by attacking; when the facilitator shows up emotionally, the impact of any misbehavior can be minimized. In that space, the covenant is less violated. When there's no competition to be right, there's less defensiveness. The process of building and posting a covenant models for people in the group a particular way of showing up. People rise to expectations. You can set the expectation of "We're grownups. We can manage this. We're going to bring our best selves. We have a lot to do. So let's do the things we need to do, and let's not waste our time having fake fights."

Covenant work is so important. It's such a beautiful opportunity that our faith provides, and it's not something that is centered in every faith. We have crafted a blessing for you as you commit to covenanting as part of the work of liberation and justice:

> May the holy be present and powerful in your covenanting process. May you know yourself accompanied by your ancestors and by the people before us who used covenant to do good work in the world. May your gathering be filled with laughter and joy, and hopefully centered on food and music and the power of community. May you move forward together knowing that this is joyful and faithful work.
>
> Amen. *Bendito Sea.*

Look at a covenant you created. What about it might you want to revisit after reading this essay?

A Welcoming Congregation Must Be Accessible

Julie Romero

What have you done to make your community, work-place, or home more accessible to more people?

When did I become someone who shows up at church once in a blue moon, a stranger to most of the community? It was not a gradual process, missing a week now and then until I was attending sporadically and finally only once in a blue moon. One day I was the religious education coordinator at a middle-sized Unitarian Universalist congregation, and the next day I was waking up in a hospital bed, hearing that my four-year-old son Myles had suffered a traumatic brain injury and was in a coma. In addition, one of my daughters, seven years old, was in traction with a fractured leg.

For obvious reasons, we did not think about going to church for many months. On the other hand, our church community worked to support our needs week after week. During the weeks I was in the hospital, and the months my son was there, we had visitors, helpers, cooks, errand runners, and hand holders from our church. Once we had settled into a routine at home, more or less, with wheelchairs, transfers, feeding, and toileting, we began venturing out into the community.

Until you need to use a wheelchair or care for someone who does, you are unlikely to see the barriers that exist to those who do. Some of the barriers we found were at the two Unitarian Universalist churches we attempted to attend.

The parish house of the church I had worked at, whose members had provided support to our family, was old. Today it has been restored, with an elevator to the second floor and a restroom that can be used by someone in a wheelchair, with room for a helper if necessary. There are curb cuts, ramps, and wide doorways. But in 1996, the year my son was injured, these did not exist. There was a ramp into the building, but the halls were narrow and the bathroom too small for a wheelchair. Church school classes were all held on the second floor, up a long flight of stairs. I did not have the energy or focus to push for the changes that were needed there. I could barely get us out the door and into the car. Some days I couldn't even do that.

A few years later my family moved to a new home near another, smaller Unitarian Universalist congregation. I knew some of the members of the congregation and started bringing my children there. This congregation met in an old VFW building, in which it rented space. You might expect that a veterans' group would have a building with good accessibility. Physical and occupational therapy had helped Myles gain mobility, and with a railing on one side and a hand to hold on the other, he was able to walk up the few steps to the entrance and then roll in to join the church school and children's activities on the first floor; but the worship space was upstairs. For a couple of years, he was able to walk up to it with assistance. As he grew taller and heavier, walking became more difficult. One day, I commented to the minister that I hoped the church would consider making changes in order to improve the building's accessibility for our congregation. She replied that there was no way do that in the rented building, and such changes would not happen until the church moved to another building. Soon after that conversation, I was sitting in the church school area with Myles. Above us, the rest of the congregation was singing. I sat with Myles and cried, feeling alone, abandoned, and angry. Since that day I have felt disconnected from church.

Accessibility has been a concern of mine since I was a young child. I was aware that there were barriers in the world if you depended on a wheelchair for your mobility. My maternal grandmother had been a quadriplegic as a result of multiple sclerosis since my mother was eight years old. My grandmother was forced to live in a hospital for the chronically ill. Once a year, if we were lucky, a relative would pay to transport her to the home of an extended family member who had a yard suited to an outdoor party. That was the only time she left the hospital for over forty years, until her death.

I was embraced by a UU congregation from the day I was born. By the time I was five years old we had moved to the South Shore of Boston, and the First Parish Church in Duxbury became my second home for almost ten years. Some of my happiest childhood memories are of experiences at that church: Christmas pageants, Thanksgiving dinners, Sunday dinners at the parsonage. Many of my childhood friends were from my church community. As a teenager, I taught Sunday school with a friend.

Another place that is home for me is Star Island, a conference center founded on the traditions of the Unitarian Universalist Association and the United Church of Christ. When

I was a child, going there meant a week to run free, reconnect with friends from far away, and feel loved by 250 people all at once. Over the years, Star Island has worked to increase its accessibility for guests. When I was a child, all of the showers were in the basement, not at all accessible. People who had difficulty with mobility couldn't access or use many of the buildings and most of the guest rooms. Now there are a few guestrooms and bathrooms, as well as several meeting rooms, that are accessible to people using wheelchairs.

When my mother, Laurel Sheridan, decided to enroll in theological school, we moved to the city to be closer to her school and to my father's job. She became an ordained Unitarian Universalist minister three years later. As a nurse turned minister, my mother was inspired to nurture spirituality in her congregation as well as help those around her feel welcome and included, and her work further embedded the importance of inclusion and accessibility in my mind. In 1997, when my mother was disabled by illness, I watched her world turn upside down. Fellow ministers told her she did not belong on retreat with them and resented the assistance she needed to participate in their group.

I now attend services occasionally. I care about many individuals in my church. I continue to identify as a Unitarian Universalist, yet I have lost the connection that would make me feel part of a congregation.

I mourn the loss often.

During the height of the pandemic, when we were housebound for weeks, I tuned in to some of the online worship services. Some people might think that online services are a great solution to the problem of accessibility. Certainly no one has a choice at the moment; we are all at home, unable to access the building. But what will happen when in-person services are possible again? My life is already one of forced partial isolation. Will my family and I be watching, on a screen, a service that everyone else is participating in? That's only a small step away from sitting downstairs listening to a congregation we can't be with. Still, I hold on to a bit of hope that in the future I will find a way to reconnect.

How do you know what the physical barriers to participation in your congregation are?

A Circle of All

Rev. Manish Mishra-Marzetti

Who do you trust?

It is April 2020. I walk into my local post office, tense and afraid. We are under "shelter in place" orders in the state of Michigan because of the novel coronavirus, and I am urgently scanning my environment: the X's marked out on the floor do not appear to be six feet apart, and the individual in front of me in line is not wearing a face covering. I find myself wondering how many people the postal service employee I talk to has interacted with; I wonder how careful those countless people have been and how many of them might be sick. Though I am a religious leader with years of spiritual practice related to deepening my sense of trust and many years of teaching and nurturing others to do the same, in this moment of risk I don't know if I can trust my environment or the other human beings within it.

While distrust and fear can drive human beings apart, it is equally true, as social psychologist Donelson Forsyth puts it in "The Psychology of Groups," that "across individuals, societies, and even eras, humans consistently seek inclusion over exclusion, membership over isolation, and acceptance over rejection" (noba.to/trfxbkhm). Our need to be with others, and to feel a sense of connection and belonging in those relationships, is as profound as, and perhaps more enduring than, any ephemeral fear that could ever grip us. Consciously and unconsciously, we look to others for recognition that we are included, worthy, and loved. Perhaps precisely because of the uncertainties and dangers that life can throw our way, we want to know who we can trust and rely on for support, love, and care. This knowing helps build a bridge of mutuality — mutual caring — which becomes the basis for belonging. This ever-present, often unspoken social process companions us on our unfolding life journey, defining painful moments of exclusion and other treasured moments of feeling cared for, valued, understood, and loved.

To whom do I belong?

"Where are you from?" This was the ubiquitous question I was greeted with throughout my childhood and adolescence in the 1970s–80s. Though I was born and raised in the United States, being a descendent of a relatively recent immigrant group meant that this question was at times a stand-in for "What's your ethnic background?" or "What is the country or nation of your cultural and racial heritage?" But the question was rarely, if ever, asked with such nuance and sophistication. It was more simply, and linguistically, presented as an other-ing: you don't look like the major racial and ethnic groups that I, the questioner, am familiar with; therefore you are not from here. So where are you from? It was also, invariably, a demand. As a child, not yet understanding all the layered nuances of the United States' history with race and ethnic-ity, I would answer "Pittsburgh" (my hometown) or "Squirrel Hill" (my neighborhood within it), and the next, almost inevi-table question would be "No, where are you *really* from? What country are you from?"

The insistence and pervasiveness of this question, throughout my youth, convinced me that I am not a child of the United States and that I didn't really belong in the U.S. The only answer that satisfied and stopped the insistent questioning was "India," and so, although I held a U.S. passport and had never lived in any country other than the U.S., the ethnic and cultural questioning directed at me convinced me, implicitly, that I was really a child of India, just somehow lost or displaced. I came to believe that I was a foreigner in my own nation of birth. This lack of belonging—this being held at arm's length as "other"—was my constant, unambiguous companion.

At the end of my junior year of high school, my father was invited to head his company's offices in New Delhi. He was concerned about displacing me during my final year of high school. I was not. I was thrilled! Finally, a chance to live in the country I was supposed to belong to—of course I wanted that! Of course not being able to graduate with peers that I had known since kindergarten was no big deal. The tantalizing prospect of fitting in, of finally belonging, was that strong.

Within months we relocated to a country I had never lived in before. I spoke English not with the British style and preferences that were dominant in India, but with a clear, unmistakable American intonation and slang. My values and mores were not those of the Indian subcontinent, but rather informed by U.S. history, experience, and culture. To my shock and surprise, invariably, as I tried to connect with Indian teenagers, somewhere early in the getting-acquainted process I would encounter a certain amount of disdain and the confounded declaration, "You're *so* American!" Rejected in

India as "too American" and a brown-skinned perpetual foreigner in the United States, belonging neither here nor there,
I was left wondering—to whom and to what did I belong?
That question, intertwined with my profound need for social
inclusion and acceptance, weighed heavily on me. In the years
and decades that followed, I have come to understand this
as a universal longing: we all want and need a sense of social
inclusion and acceptance. We all want to know, and trust, that
we belong.

Laying claim to belonging

My life experience has shown me that I need to almost stub-
bornly claim where I belong. After graduating high school in
India, I returned to the United States absolutely clear that I
would never again allow anyone to treat me as if the United
States were not my country, as if I were a foreigner in my
own nation. This involved a shift in the locus of my sense of
belonging. Belonging is inherently a relational concept, and
yet I had to be able to lay claim to it myself and hold on to
that claim with love and fierce conviction. The United States
is far from perfect. It is a deeply flawed nation—there are
many things about its history and structures that I view as
immoral and reject—and yet it is my nation. I belong to it,
and it belongs to me. No human being can affirm my birth-
right more than my U.S. birth certificate already does. In
equal measure, I am a child of India's religions, languages,
art, music, cinema, cuisine, and sartorial style. There is no
entity that can vouch that parts of me "authentically" belong
to Indian culture. I have had to reach out and lay claim to
my sense of belonging to both the U.S. and India. I am an

American of Indian heritage—in between and of both. No one can decide otherwise for me.

My journey within Unitarian Universalism has some parallels. I found our tradition in my late twenties. I arrived carrying baggage that was rooted in disappointment with the version of Hinduism I had been raised with. As a result, I rejected certain religious ideas, concepts, and rituals. I was angry and resentful toward the concept of God; I rejected all forms of prayer as petitioning for, and/or expecting, supernatural intervention. Human possibility was what I had faith in. It was what I trusted. It was all I needed. My early experiences of Unitarian Universalism were quite affirming. The experience of being in communal relationships of intentional learning and growth fostered my evolution. I began to heal and to develop my own understanding of Unitarian Universalism.

I began redefining language, concepts, and rituals in ways that made sense to me and felt empowering and uplifting. This emerging syncretism was still decidedly Unitarian Universalist, but it was increasingly my *interpretation* of Unitarian Universalism. I saw echoes and pieces of my personal interpretation in the lives of other Unitarian Universalists, but my version was my own. Over the years, I came to wonder if I was still Unitarian Universalist. Had I, in developing my own interpretation of the tradition, outgrown it? Was it too narrow to accommodate the place I had reached, or too wide and shallow to allow the depth I sought? And underneath all this wondering was a persistent question: "Do I still belong in Unitarian Universalism?"

Appropriately, the answer to this question emerged in community with others, specifically in a dialogue with a congregant. This congregant echoed all the same questions that I periodically asked myself: "Do I still belong within Unitarian Universalism? Is there room here for me? Am I valued? Am I seen? What about all the people who relate to this tradition in ways that are very different from how I do? Isn't that a sign that I don't belong here?" My answer was, "Of course you belong here—as long as you *choose* to belong here and are aligned with our basic tenets and understandings (which are about as religiously progressive as it gets, and fairly minimalistic in what they specify). No one is going to deliver you a feeling of belonging on a silver platter. But if you lay claim to it—to belonging—if you decide that this tradition is yours as much as it is anyone else's, then you belong, and you will belong for as long as you choose to belong. Whatever your beliefs, perspectives, interests, or activities, not everyone within Unitarian Universalism will agree with you or share your interests. We are too broad a tradition for uniform agreement on anything. But there will always be some others who have experiences, interests, perspectives, and needs similar to yours. That can be enough. We don't need to make everyone else just like us in order to belong. But you do have to claim the belonging that is yours to claim." The insights of my young adult years reemerged in a new light, pointing toward how I, and others, might have a sense of belonging within Unitarian Universalism.

I invite you to think about the phrase "lay claim to" that I've used, with its implications of grabbing, of asserting ownership. On one hand, such a phrase connotes self-empowerment. On the other hand, one can—and should—ask why such self-empowerment is necessary. Why does a sense of belonging sometimes need to be wrested from social structures or other people? Why is it treated as currency, as power, as defining in-groups and out-groups?

In your community, to whom is belonging easily conferred? By extension, to whom is belonging rarely conferred or conferred with greater difficulty?

Building Sacred Cyberspace

Linnea Nelson

Which kinds of online experiences have created a sense of community for you?

A retired woman in our congregation sought out my husband every Sunday for "her hug." These physical connections, along with the smiles, the shared tears, the nods of recognition and enthusiastic waves from across the sanctuary, were all part of how we built relationships in our faith communities before the COVID-19 pandemic. These physical movements helped us stay healthy and connected. When the pandemic began, some panic and much consternation ensued . . . and we couldn't reach out to our Unitarian Universalist friends in person. We wondered how we would stay in touch, provide comfort, and serve our communities as we lived out our faith when we couldn't be physically together.

Religious professionals worried about congregants' need to be together, be in worship, and be able to serve and learn together. Unitarian Universalist clergy and staff immediately explored the technology that could bring us together for worship, connection, and learning. Creative solutions were hastily shared online through professional networks and social media.

No longer was it a question of whether we could create sacred space online; we needed to make it happen now!

Religious professionals, staff, and lay leaders rallied their collective skills and created worship, religious education, coffee hours, and other small group ministries online. Music, stories, readings, lessons, and poetry were graciously shared. Black Lives of Unitarian Universalism (BLUU) and the Church of the Larger Fellowship (CLF) were already adept at leading online worship and offered a helping hand to those boldly stepping into this space.

Religious professionals needed support as they navigated this new way forward. The stress of new learning, often through trial and error, and of spending many hours online led many to feel tired and even overwhelmed by the multitude of tasks at hand. And, of course, technology did not always cooperate. Unitarian Universalist religious professionals spontaneously formed groups in order to engage, hold space for one another, and listen deeply to the trials and successes of this new era. Like the weekly and monthly groups that formed for members and friends of congregations, online small groups for religious professionals also appeared—to check in, care for one another, and create a space for grieving, loneliness, and support. The Unitarian Universalist Ministers Association (UUMA) opened its sessions to all religious professionals, inviting them to experience ritual and worship together. Listening to the cares and concerns of the participants was key to the rituals. The Liberal Religious Educators Association (LREDA) supported religious educators with a regular time to connect online, share spiritual practices, commiserate, and share successes. A LREDA group specifically for BIPOC people (Black, Indigenous, and People of Color) was formed, since separation and oppression intersected to bring additional challenges to ministry.

In our race to hold ourselves together, worship, conduct meetings, socialize, and keep our families engaged, we first needed to focus on the technical requirements. Church staff, religious professionals, and congregants learned new technological language and taught each other how to download, install, and use unfamiliar software. Together we learned to create, stream, and record worship services, small group ministry events, and social media videos. Religious education teachers, many of whom were more familiar with video streaming and social media than other religious professionals, found new ways to connect with class members. People also stayed in touch through email, phone calls, and letters. Some offered stories and meditations, others take-home activities with personal notes to children and youth. Everyone was scrambling to adjust to the changing circumstances.

I wondered whether Unitarian Universalists were also going to take advantage of this opportunity. How would worship change? How would we increase engagement with our faith? What did families need to feel included? What did newcomers need? Would we learn things about ourselves that would have taken decades to learn without the pandemic? Would we tap into an entirely new culture of worship, service, and relationship in our faith?

Some of these online groups, classes, and worship services blossomed, while others withered. What was the key to the former's success?

Although there are many paths to sustainable online experiences, joining other members of my congregation in an online UU Wellspring small group ministry program led me to the sacred space that I was yearning for. UU Wellspring is a yearlong spiritual deepening program for Unitarian

Universalists that crafts sacred space by taking an intentional approach to learning how to listen well, engage in spiritual practice, and learn how to develop a UU lens. For me, learning how to practice deep listening has been the most important key to making online groups sustainable. In UU Wellspring, participants learn to listen without judgment and without attempting to fix or advise others. This allows them to speak from their hearts. We also learn how to pause to discuss harm when it occurs. During our sessions online, just as when we were in person, I saw people breathing more easily and settling into just *being*. There was a sense of slowing down, knowing that the UU Wellspring process would allow everyone to be fully heard, as we discussed materials that often led to profound moments of learning and discovery. Deep listening brought the sacred space we were yearning for in what had become a new normal.

Participation in the small group ministry programs of UU Wellspring deeply connected me to the participants in the group, my congregation, and my faith. The deep listening that was taught, haggled, and practiced there soon led us to forge a bold space where we could share ideas that were new to us while others listened without judgment. We learned vulnerability and deep connection with our own souls, as well as deep engagement with one another. We learned to speak our truths, knowing that our words were being held and not judged, listened to and not questioned. Some kind of enchantment prevailed in every UU Wellspring circle, and deep listening seemed to be at the heart of it. At almost every session someone would comment that this group was their anchor or that it allowed them to move through the pandemic with more grace and gratitude.

I believe the reason the program functioned so well in online sessions was deep listening to both the words *and* the sacred silent spaces between our words. The online format, in which people muted their microphones when they were not speaking, supported our slow, contemplative conversations about the meaning behind the words as we explored what it means to be a Unitarian Universalist. The practice of muting and unmuting also promoted moments of contemplation between speakers, allowed speakers to complete their thoughts, and made it easier for them to pause while speaking. By not muting themselves, they could indicate that they were not finished or that they needed a moment of silence before the next person spoke. Reciprocally, other participants learned to unmute, to show that they were ready to speak, while still remaining silent, inviting a moment of sacred space to allow the first speaker's ideas to settle. What a luxury!

When sacred space was secured through the commitment to deep listening in these yearlong groups, each person's soul somehow found the will to speak in the group. Whether from the wisdom of ancestors, through personal experiences and beliefs, or by reading the assignments through a Unitarian Universalist lens, participants listened and learned from each other without the judgment or questioning usually found in everyday conversations. Parker Palmer's admonition "No fixing, no saving, no setting each other straight" created a space for participants to become vulnerable and to accept one another's joys and challenges. Importantly, UU Wellspring also teaches us to be "holy disrupters," charging us to notice and intervene when something is said that brings harm to others. This aspect of deep listening creates a boundary that encompasses the sacred space and allows us to be called back into covenant rather than perpetuating harm, even unknowingly.

I also loved hearing the clear voices in my headphones; headphones can help those with hearing difficulties participate more fully. The occasional momentary screen freeze offered a moment of grace as the group patiently waited for reconnection and gently offered space for repeating any interrupted reflections. I often asked groups to use any technological glitch as a reminder to take a few cleansing breaths and to see it as a gift of a peaceful moment. Together we honored both our reflections and our silences, even when they were unexpected; maybe the online format meant we honored them more. It was clear that, as long as we were intentional about it, deep listening was achievable online. Once deep listening is established, online communities can fully focus on engagement. Young adults have been connecting online, through gaming and social media, for most of their lives, and some of them faced the pandemic lockdown with relative equanimity. They provided a good model of online connection and engagement.

We were all looking for community, for connection to each other and to our faith. No longer could we just arrive at church and be fed a message. Active online engagement meant being fully present, and many of our worship services, classes, fellowship opportunities, and justice work events encouraged congregational voices to be heard. Since true engagement requires presence, speaking, holding space for others, and deeply listening to one another, many congregations focused on these aspects once they had established the basics of using a platform like Zoom, Facebook Live, or YouTube. I started to see a multitude of ways in which congregations were engaging their members and creating community in cyberspace: congregants shared joys and sorrows in chat boxes, families of all configurations lit and extinguished chalices, and congregants provided all sorts of music and readings. Some congregations shared photos or short videos at the beginning or end of services, and these touches brought personal engagement to our worship spaces.

We don't yet know the full impact of this online engagement. The pandemic crisis has opened up new ways of connecting and guiding our spiritual lives, developing our Unitarian Universalist identities, creating social justice initiatives, and leaning into areas we can affect in our communities.

Deep listening and intentional, active engagement created sacred space for our souls to speak. If we continue to focus on developing the practice of deep listening and joining to engage meaningfully with one another in our Unitarian Universalist communities, we just might construct the spiritual power needed to become relevant to both our members and the world. And perhaps, by building deep listening skills and intentionally engaging one another online, we can share the virtual hugs we have been yearning for.

How can you bring deep listening and more intentional engagement to your online programs?

A Constellation of Care for All Genders

Rev. Theresa I. Soto

Where do you process your learning about antioppression?

It is easy to mistake keeping rules for keeping covenant, but keeping covenant is not only more than, but also different from, obeying rules. As Dr. Rebecca Parker says, "there is a Universal Love that has never broken faith with us and never will." Keeping covenant means holding one another in light of that love. Although we make mistakes, our love and our practices of love matter in the long term.

How can we treat each other with care and inclusion? One way is by learning, using, and respecting the pronouns each person uses for themselves. But pronoun use is just one star in what should be an entire constellation of care. Let us examine some others.

Learn Trans 101 information without practicing on trans or nonbinary people.

Students learning to drive must read the drivers' handbook and understand what's involved in handling a car. In the same way, people who are just beginning to learn about trans and nonbinary issues should begin by gaining basic vocabulary and some understanding of how to use it appropriately and kindly. One way to start learning about trans people is by joining a reading and practice group, whose members can support one another, share resources, and grow together, both in skills and in their resolve to act with compassion.

Pay attention to the way your congregation both affirms and doesn't affirm trans and nonbinary folks and their lives and experiences.

We are a faith and ethics movement that leads strongly with the idea that every person matters. When you think about the work you want to do to create welcome and to build community, one of the important questions to ask yourself is, "In what ways does my congregation assume that every person listening, participating, or leading is either a cisgender man or a woman?" Whether individual or collective, these assumptions create an experience of erasure, which Parul Sehgal defines as "the practice of collective indifference that renders certain people and groups invisible" ("Fighting 'Erasure,'" www.nytimes.com/2016/02/07/magazine/the-painful -consequences-of-erasure.html).

That experience of erasure, of being rendered invisible, makes people weary of trying to be seen, weary especially of asking for care and inclusion that are already freely available to others. Erasure is encountered in hymn lyrics that speak only of men and women, in physical spaces such as restrooms that may be formally or informally made unwelcoming for trans and nonbinary congregants, and in the language surrounding men's and women's retreats, which excludes nonbinary participants and leaves trans men and women guessing whether they will be accepted there.

An affirming congregation, on the other hand, actively and vocally welcomes all its members. It provides non-gendered physical spaces such as all-gender restrooms, includes trans, nonbinary, and gender-expansive people in its bylaws, and fosters a culture of asking for rather than assuming pronouns and other personal information.

Some people may argue that noticing and caring about people who are different from the dominant culture is basing too much on identity. But not doing so is a choice; it is not a matter of dogma. Doing so is also a choice, and we should choose to care about people, because people matter. And our Universalist traditions, together with our generosity of spirit, make clear to us that when we say that everyone matters, we do not mean only the people we already know and understand.

Be supportive of trans and nonbinary folks in and out of the congregation.

Consider that practical and financial support from the congregation can benefit both the givers and the recipients. Financial support for people who are going through the expensive process of transitioning can help them feel included in and affirmed by their ethical and spiritual home. Other forms of support include using liturgy by trans and nonbinary folks, sharing messages of belonging at Pride events, educational events such as college fairs, and even social events. One supportive thing that anyone can do is to *listen to trans and nonbinary people*. Listen to what people say they want and need. Attempts to provide what we think someone needs aren't helpful if what the person truly needs is something else.

Remember that gender is only one part of identity and that people's identities have many intersecting elements.

Gender is only one part of a person's identity. Our identities also include elements like race and ethnicity, class, age, and other social and economic factors, and all of these affect how we are treated. All the parts of us need to be liberated. A congregation that is antiracist but misogynist still has work to do in affirming that everyone matters and everyone belongs.

This is an excerpt from a poem called "dear trans*, non-binary, genderqueer, and gender-expansive friends and kin: (and those of us whose gender is survival)" in my book *Spilling the Light*. It is part of a blessing for trans and nonbinary people and others. I wonder if you can open your heart to imagine wrapping trans and nonbinary folks in the care of this blessing. Imagine that care for yourself. A constellation of care goes beyond pronouns to establishing more love for each and all of us.

> *your stories belong to you.*
> *your joy and complexity is beautiful,*
> *however you may choose to tell it (or not*
> *tell it). some folks (cis) may take their liberty*
> *for an unholy license. you are beloved. please*
> *keep to our shared tasks of*
> *healing*
> *getting free.*

How does your community prioritize trans and nonbinary inclusion? What learning needs to happen, and how are the opportunities for learning unfolding?

Beyond the "Both/And"

Rev. Leslie Takahashi

What assumptions do you find people often make about you in your community?

I have a manual typewriter on which I wrote my senior thesis in college. Though it was not electric, it had a mechanism that allowed the spacing to proceed at a rapid pace, which was pretty special at the time. The typewriter is in my garage now, up on a high shelf in its black plastic case. I think it will be something fun for when my grandchildren are old enough to mess with such things.

I have had experiences with that machine I will never have with others: my thesis, letters home from college (because then as now, my handwriting is unreadable), early short stories, and I think even part of my first attempt at a novel. And yet I can't rely on that typewriter as my primary mode of capturing my thoughts anymore. Now I use computers, my phone, and even a digital recording device. My use of these would probably not be possible if I hadn't first had the experience with that little typewriter.

I was in my early thirties when I first heard the concept of "both/and" thinking. It became one of the pillars of my spiritual life. To move out of the dichotomy, out of the binary choice of "either/or," is to enter a whole new way of being. Doing so transformed my life. And now, as we reemerge into this familiar/unfamiliar, known/unknown, hopeful/despairing world of 2021, I am realizing that my old friend is necessary and not sufficient, a bit like the old typewriter—an important step in the journey but not the final destination.

First, I want to sing the praises of my old friend "both/ and" for a while.

The ability to hold two truths that may seem contradictory is still a superpower. Doing so allows us to comprehend that no single truth exists and that it is within the intersections of many that we often find the most intriguing glimmerings of truth. This era of false news, in which a few pixels can create supposed truths the way fairytales made gold from straw, means that we have to understand that something can be simultaneously objectively false and also very convincing and motivating for people who believe it. It is both true that those who are older (and I grow more so each year) have wisdom gleaned from the passage of time and also true that, especially now, those just entering young adulthood have the clearest understanding of the world and its problems. Both true: democracy is a critical value for us as Unitarian Universalists, and we have to re-evaluate how to exercise it in our congregations.

I think of the relationship between each side of the both/ and as joined rather than separated, the way Ranier Marie Rilke talks about love: "Love consists of this: two solitudes that meet, protect and greet each other."

As a mixed-race person, I have always lived in a both/ and world—and not necessarily with love on either side for the other, even within my own personhood. Back in the day, antiracism trainings used to invite us to think of the first person we had met who was of a different race from ourselves. For me, that was my mother. As the product of two people each from a xenophobic culture, I understood from my youngest days that I was "mixed." While I value the nicer-sounding "multiracial" that came later in my experience, I experienced all the complications of "mixed." I was neither English-ancestors-on-the-Mayflower proper nor insulated-Japanese-American-community proper. Neither culture was highlighted or celebrated for me—except by one work colleague of my father's, who kept telling me to be proud of the Japanese culture my father was trying so hard to erase in those days. Because of this fracture, I took only small pieces of these inheritances such as my grandmother's love of English literature and childhood Unitarian stories and my father's eventual exploration of Japanese art and ceramics.

"Both/and" made so much sense to me that I began a practice many years ago of never using the word "or." By being conscious of when I almost chose that small and powerful divider, I also became more aware of the ways that multiple truths can embrace one another. The both/and-ness of conflicts between millennials and boomers around me, who saw their futures, their rights, and their concerns about issues such as racial reconciliation and climate change through such different lenses, made sense—the dance between hope and despair. I can find ways to engage in antiracism work and the work of cultural honoring while understanding that two contradictory ideas/experiences/ways of being can both contain truth.

To get our dominant culture to even consider this idea instead of arguing every disagreement to death is critical, hard, and often still impossible. We are so programmed to choose the either/or that our teaching and preaching, cajoling and extoling don't seem to make much headway.

Yet, my old friend is . . . dated.

In recent years, I have started noticing that being limited to "both/and" is no longer sufficient for the complexities we face. There are often more than two truths we need to hold at once—for example, the truths of millennials, Gen X, Gen Z, and boomers. Or the emotions that the young adults inheriting this very beautiful and disturbed and terrifying world have to walk through every day. Or the relationship among the many challenging issues that face us—that climate change is related to racism and classism and ableism and hyper-capitalism, for example.

The old rule I was taught is that "between" involves two parties while "among" is three or more. We are so much in an "among" world now. I don't have a new term I truly like, but "multi/and" comes closest to capturing this emphasis on multiple truths rather than exactly two.

So how do we learn to lead and live among "multi/and" truths when so many of us are still doing the work to embrace the "both/and"? Perhaps that question itself is a sign of the times and of the complicated relationships we need to be able to hold.

Many people have already learned to navigate multiple ways of being and moving through the world. Gender expansive people have a sophisticated understanding of the complexities of living multiple truths. Multiracial people—both those younger than I and some of us "mixed" oldsters—also understand, as do disabled people and transracial adoptees who live within the frames of multiple cultures. I am grateful for their teachings.

So I guess I will make a new friend ("multi/and") and keep the old ("both/and"), since to dwell among them is to have insight into this world. Perhaps our congregations can become places where we understand that those who know pain also know great joy; that we can be peoples celebrating minds and bodies and spirits; that families come in many forms; and that friendship can comfort and challenge and expand us.

We need these friends to survive.

People who watch such things are predicting that the pandemic will hasten the demise of organized religious life in the United States. One reason I believe many organized religions are struggling is their insistence on unilateral truths among multi/and realities. One cannot force a single doctrine that emerged from a societal monoculture to fit into the multiple truth, multi-modality world we live in now.

In fact, unilateral truths never did work for all, probably not even for most. Those people who assured me as a teen that I could "pass for white" did not understand the landscape of my inner world. Those of us who pine for a "simpler world" do not understand that that world excluded more people than it included.

And our faith, our precious Unitarian Universalism, is not immune to this. How often do we wrestle with each other because someone has nostalgia for a world that only existed for people like them?

So what is our work in service of and living among the "multi/and"?

Perhaps it is to practice questioning more than answering, listening more than questioning, learning more than knowing. Perhaps it is to drag out a slightly unordered collection of truths into our tidy sanctuaries on Sunday mornings and not be afraid if the whole mess isn't detangled 2000 words later. Perhaps it is being there to say, "I don't know the answer, but

I will still be with you in your pain," and not shunning those whose complexities defy our easy molds. Personally, I find solace in learning from those who live in this complexity on a daily basis and letting their wisdom be a guide. Perhaps it is to honor that those who came before us, those who lead now, and those who will come after us all bear truths and that all those truths are worth carrying.

I know this: I still prefer the world of "and" to the world of "or." And now I am trying to learn to expand my reach to include as many truths as possible and to hold them against each other to see what new wisdom emerges.

Perhaps these words from Alice Walker's "The Gospel According to Shug" hint toward the world we need to bring into being:

HELPED are those who love all the colors of all the human beings, as they love all the colors of the animals and plants; none of their children, nor any of their ancestors, nor any parts of themselves, shall be hidden from them.

HELPED are those who love the lesbian, the gay, and the straight, as they love the sun, the moon, and the stars. None of their children, nor any of their ancestors, nor any parts of themselves, shall be hidden from them.

HELPED are those who love the broken and the whole; none of their children, nor any of their ancestors, nor any parts of themselves, shall be hidden from them.

May all of this be enough truth for these days.

What common phrases or assumptions could be reframed as "both/and" or "multi/and" in your community?

The Magic Pool of UU Youth Culture

L. C. Magee

What are your own memories of community as a youth?

Here is what I don't exactly remember from my time as a Unitarian Universalist high school youth:

The weekly schedules. The exact seating arrangements of the couches in our strangely polyhedral youth group room. The sleepy ten hours of a car trip to and from a youth convention. All the policies of the youth–adult committee over four years of meetings. Some finer details of a United Nations panel, a church-sponsored trip to learn about and discuss systematic wealth inequality. Most of a convention I spent resting in a post-bronchitis haze, in 102° summer Baltimore heat in a church with no AC, before I emerged at sunset, having sweated my sickness out. I do remember, though, that a friend put his hand on my shoulder and said seriously, happily, "You look a lot better."

Here is what else I remember:

I am fourteen and in a linoleum-floored campground dining hall courtesy of Cape Henlopen State Park. The rest of the youth group are filtering about, playing Uno and Risk and Capture the Flag. But I'm sitting at a table with the other youth–adult committee members and our youth ministry coordinator. In front of us are a couple of scraps of notebook paper on which to sketch out a youth-led worship. This meeting is meant to remind us of the covenant we're bringing to this space. It's an opportunity to do our own preaching, to speak to our peers directly instead of listening, as we've always done, to an adult. I'm interested in this because I like organization and asking deep questions, and I have a general sense that writing is something I enjoy. We brainstorm a theme and some potential opening words, and I suggest a song: "We Didn't Start the Fire."

Heads start nodding. To my surprise, the others build on this, quickly figuring out the rest of the worship to have it ready by the time our team-cooked dinner is served. This moment is one of the first in a long series of formative experiences that being a Unitarian Universalist youth gave me: acknowledgment. *Oh,* I thought, *they're listening to me.* I was a clinically depressed teen attending a high school known more for its suicide rates than its sports teams, and I began to realize that church was a place where people actually wanted to hear what I had to say. Where the adults, and much more importantly, my peers, would not only think of me but reach out for my opinion.

Liberal religion brings with it an acceptance not only of our social differences but also of our struggles. All the most intense and rewarding conversations I've had in a church-related space began with familiarity and comfort. In youth group, barriers broke down because we had fun together, cooked and goofed off and planned our activities. Nothing needed to be too serious, and anything forced felt stilted and inauthentic. Eventually the easy haze of friendship descended. It was okay to be vulnerable because here you were safe.

These moments of vulnerability still are among my most vivid memories because they ring the most true. I can still see a peer walking out of his own worship crying—a poem had hit too hard. Conversations in darkened pod rooms ranged from whether God exists to gender expression to stories of self-harm and the quiet terror of getting older.

Regional youth cons were advertised to me as a place to meet other Unitarian Universalist kids outside my home congregation. At first, I didn't understand—or, to be honest, much enjoy—cons. They were packed with kids who formed tight-knit groups that, although they didn't mean to be exclusionary, were difficult to find my way into. My first con was in summer, and it was one that hosted its own unique bridging ceremony each year. I watched as seniors cried as they gave their speeches. This display of how the community had deeply touched each of them was baffling to me, someone just entering the space.

What was so special here that I was missing, I wondered? So I kept coming back, curious and learning. A year later and by pure chance, on a couch in Delaware County, I met one of the best friends I've ever had. And I began to truly understand why the youth community was so special.

Everyone who came to cons was interesting. Those who wanted to play could play. Those who wanted to talk could talk. No one shamed another for not understanding the purpose of the shared space. The atmosphere at cons took the wonderful inclusivity of youth group to an entirely different level. I've seen the unexplainable, magical, all-permeating feeling described as the "magic pool": a space deeply and reverently respectful, sacred and vulnerable, loving.

At one of the first youth-led worships I ever attended, we held hands to walk in a loop around the room before sitting in a wide circle. There were two youth leading, a dark room, a single tea light in the center as our chalice. I recall how unexpectedly the format affected me, made me aware of the bonds between us. How it made me aware that all of our shared spaces, no matter how casual, are places of spiritual experience. Eventually I took on the job of worship chair for regional youth cons.

My own bridging ceremony at a Unitarian Universalist–affiliated summer camp, Unirondack, felt like the last hurrah of my youth experience. It was the welcoming culture of a con packed into a week of outdoor living. Here is what I remember: sobbing into my best friend's shirt after singing to a firelit room of over fifty people. Because it had sunk in that I had to move on. That no one could predict what the future held.

I knew that young adult spaces existed, and after high school I was increasingly interested in trying them out. After all, the traditional church services that I had been told were the next step felt strangely foreign. They weren't unpleasant, but they were oddly disconnected from the Unitarian Universalist world I'd known so far. I was still in touch with many people I'd met up and down the East Coast, so I decided to synch bus tickets with my best friend for a young adult con in Binghamton. I wasn't expecting it to be exactly the same, and it wasn't, but from the first hours in I knew that what I loved wasn't lost.

The bridgers who organize and attend their own young adult cons are the ones who were most involved in their youth communities. We are the ones responsible for keeping our own flame alive. To my intense joy I discovered that it was possible for young adults to build the kinds of radically inclusive spaces that reflected what I loved about Unitarian Universalism. It was still possible to have fun, discuss social justice initiatives, and talk about the larger questions of life with people who really understood me. People who would reach out and listen.

To my absolute delight, there was a young-adult—planned worship, which was just as spiritually fulfilling as I had hoped. After that, nearly everyone present joined in on the traditional group "coffeehouse," sharing a song or dance or improv comedy. The fun allowed me to understand my peers even more fully.

Although I hadn't written a proper worship in two years, I once again thought about my own growing call to ministry and possible future religious studies. This was the type of church I wanted to bring to people. The atmosphere of love I know is possible for anyone who needs it.

It is important to recognize that these worships were strong, spiritually deep, and collaborative experiences, yet they tended to be far away from what most congregants think of as worship. Young adults and youth may meet up in churches and enjoy services, but the majority of our spiritual and personal growth happens in unstructured conversations and play areas outside what is traditionally thought of as a church service.

So I'm left feeling that something is lacking when I'm sitting in a pew. Is this the "next step"? Is this the adulthood I was waiting for? I think, "When do we get to talk to each other?"

Here is the general setup of a church (or congregation, or fellowship, or gathering) that I've pieced together from twenty-four voluntary Unitarian Universalist youth and young adult events over six years: above you there are beams, a vaulted ceiling, perhaps some tasteful stained glass if you're in New York. We seem to be fond of community-knit tapestries and paint handprints. And the chairs, anywhere from a dozen to hundreds of them, or perhaps instead there are wooden pews left over from Christianity. Maybe there is a pulpit, or at least a dais one step up, with places for the clergy to sit. What's always immediately clear is that these are separate areas: here is the congregation, and here is the minister. And in this space you sit to learn a lesson to carry out into the wider world in faith and love and go-in-peace. Stand as you are willing and able. Listen. Outside, off the main hallway, there is usually a room with a linoleum floor where the coffee is made, and there, at the designated hour, we can take the time to talk to each other. The church service that happens here is an old and often satisfying ritual, but it induces a bit of culture shock if you're not used to it, if your experience as a youth does not match what you're expected to love as an adult.

There's nothing wrong with the traditional church format; it has clearly been effective for hundreds of years. There is much to be gained from the lessons of the past. But among those friends I've written worships with and been enlightened by, I see little drive or motivation to give to "adult" spaces. It is genuinely disorienting to attend church on Sunday, because the Unitarian Universalist community there is structured so differently, and operates so differently, from the one I've grown to love. The youth and young adult format that we ourselves cultivated is much more rewarding. I've heard from others on this issue, discussed it at length, seen a blog post or two that describes the feeling in more eloquent words than I can pen here. It feels good to sit in community and sing with the congregation, to listen to a minister and understand the lesson. To see the beams above me. But my God needs no structure. And the only part of the service I look forward to is the part when we really begin to interact.

The Unitarian Universalist community I know has been intensely rewarding socially, spirituality, and developmentally. But, like many others, I cannot connect with a larger Unitarian Universalist space until it makes efforts to adapt to its own youth culture. Time and time again I see committees wondering how to attract younger families and decrease the steep drop-off in involvement we see after the bridging ceremony. And I think, "Have you made an effort to understand them?"

Conversation requires community requires trust. I promise: we want to be in Beloved Community with you too.

How do you measure the degree to which the youth of your community trust that community? How might you increase or expand their trust?

Kids Talk About Community

Nichole Hodges-Abbasi, Zachi Abbasi (age 10),
and Tobi Abbasi (age 9)

What does community mean to you?

When religious educator Nichole Hodges-Abbasi asked her nine- and ten-year-old children, "What does community mean to you?" the conversation that followed was filled with honest observations.

Zachi, ten years old, grounded his answer in his congregation: "Community is a bigger group of people that do the same thing and honor or believe in the same thing." Since Zachi attends both a mosque and the Unitarian Universalist Congregation of Frederick, Maryland, Nichole asked further, "When you go to the Unitarian Universalist Congregation of Frederick, do you feel community?"

Zachi enthusiastically answered, "Yes, I hear Reverend Carl talk about it all the time, like 'We are a beloved community.'"

"So, Rev. Carl says that, but do you *feel* it?"

"I feel it," Zachi said. "I feel like I just really connect with my friends and that they can help me sometimes and they're never mean or say mean things. They just help you when you need help, and you help them when they need help. I feel like I'm in a community with them. It's not like school.

Everyone likes each other. They're open to thinking, and so they're there to be kind to one another."

Nichole asked, "Are there any other places where you feel a sense of community?"

"School community, or my town, I guess." Zachi pondered. "I feel community lots of places. I feel community sometimes even in the woods, where it seems like there's no one and maybe there are creatures less than an inch away from you. I feel it in nature."

Children often have spiritual moments that go unquestioned by adults. Zachi embodies the web of life through his connections with the people in his communities and with nature. The Unitarian Universalist Seventh Principle honors the web of life, and Zachi clearly feels connected to both the people and creatures in his life.

"Do you ever feel community when you go to pray at the mosque with your cousins?" wondered Nichole.

"I feel welcome there. Everyone is saying *Assalamualaikum*, which means 'hello' and 'peace be with you' in Urdu and in Arabic."

"Are there any differences between the mosque and the Unitarian Universalist Congregation of Frederick?"

"They don't judge at the mosque, just like Unitarian Universalists. They never judge another religion. Never judge another person."

Zachi has captured the Unitarian Universalist First Principle of affirming the dignity of all lives. His connection to two faiths allows him to bring his whole self to Unitarian Universalism. Attending a congregation where they can bring all of themselves, not just the parts that meet certain expectations, allows people to fully belong.

Zachi continues, "They dress differently and speak differently, though."

Zachi, at his tender age, notices the similarities before the differences. His observation that he feels unjudged in both places indicates a way of fully welcoming all to Unitarian Universalism. How people feel in a Unitarian Universalist community is paramount to their ability to engage fully and embody their faith as Unitarian Universalists.

"Let's talk about how we treat one another, because that is really important. What are some ways that our Unitarian Universalist congregation shows how we want to treat one another?

"We are a welcoming congregation."

"Can you say more about what that means? Do you have an example of it?"

Nine-year-old Tobi has been patiently waiting for a turn to share his observations; now he suggests that gender-neutral bathrooms are an important way to be inclusive.

Nichole agrees with him. "You know, Tobi, that is a really good point! The signs definitely help let our congregation and visitors know that they are free to use any bathroom that meets their needs—just be sure to wash your hands!" Then she invites Zachi to respond as well: "Zachi, what do you think makes us a welcoming congregation?"

"They give you name tags each week so you can decide if you want to be a member," he says. "They give you a red one if you are new and you want to try it out. Then if you see someone with a white name tag, that means they have been a member of the church for a while, so you can have a conversation with them. And even if you're just going to the congregation because you want to go there, it's still okay."

Congregations that add pronouns to name tags make their space welcoming in still another way. Children who grow up with gender-neutral restrooms and pronoun identification in their communities see that they, and people of all genders and gender expressions, are valued and belong.

Belonging requires connection, so Nichole asks her boys, "What is the thing that you're doing at the Unitarian Universalist Congregation of Frederick where you feel the greatest sense of connection?"

"When you're playing with all of your friends and creating games," replies Zachi.

"So you feel the greatest sense of community when you're playing?"

"Yeah. One more thing, when you're like me in fifth grade, at my school you don't get to see other groups. You have your lunch time with only your own class and your recess with the same people every day, without kids of different ages. At church, you get to see friends who are other ages."

Tobi adds, "Sometimes I feel it when we're playing, and sometimes I feel it during the service."

Nichole queries, "During the 'Story for All Ages,' Tobi?"

"When I get to sit with all of my friends, especially my best friends. I wish all of my friends came every time. I like it more when all my friends come."

"That makes sense. Thanks, guys!"

What would you say are three core ways of building community in a congregation?

Worshipping in Fullness and Truth as Black UUs

Rev. Mykal O'Neal Slack

What do you hope for in Unitarian Universalist worship services?

"Hey! How long will worship be today?"

The question was not an unfamiliar one for me, but it struck me as odd in the moment. Most of the 115 or so people who had converged on All Souls Kansas City in April 2018 for Black Lives of Unitarian Universalism's first-ever revival, appropriately titled *Reclaim!*, had just begun to gather for breakfast. It was Saturday morning, the only full day of a revival weekend that had begun Friday afternoon and that would end after worship on Sunday. And while we had a full day of programming ahead, nobody was talking about the program, the guest speakers and preachers, or the breaks. Folks seemed focused on and grateful for the most important things—good food, good conversation, connections, and community.

The person had rushed toward me, nearly spilling her coffee, to ask her question. And her approach and tone made it abundantly clear to me that there was a right answer and that she was really hoping I knew what that right answer was. I could see from her name badge that she had traveled far to get to this gathering, and the success of her whole trip seemed to hang on how I might respond. Imagine the look of awe on her face when I said, "As long or as short as it needs to be." With widened eyes and an eagerly nodding head, she shouted, "Aaaahhh, very good," and went on about her way.

When I asked her later about her question, she said that it had probably come out of a mix of things, which she ultimately summed up as excited curiosity about what worship would be like among us, Black UUs and Black UU-adjacent folks, in this setting of revival, a setting she had never experienced as a UU. It was an understandable curiosity, particularly since many Black folks in BLUU's growing spiritual family often describe worship in predominantly white UU settings as "stale" and "lackluster." And she wasn't alone in her wondering. None of us, not even those of us on the worship team, really knew what to expect, but we did know that a meaningful place to start was with the concept of revival.

When BLUU announced that *Reclaim!* would be happening in Kansas City, Missouri, we knew people across our shared faith would wonder why we would choose to host a revival in mid-America. My friend and colleague Dr. Takiyah Nur Amin, who served as BLUU's content director at the time, and I explained that revival, at its core, is a resurgence of something, a recovering of something that gives abundant life and unwavering hope at a time when those things might otherwise seem out of reach and even unimaginable. Revival, for BLUU, is about revising and reimagining Unitarian Universalism's commitment to embodying Beloved Community in a real, tangible way. Too much had happened, both in the United States and within Unitarian Universalism, and our folks were hungry for something community oriented and spiritually grounding. We needed a space to just be and be fed, to connect and to recalibrate. BLUU spaces are always deeply relational, culturally rich, and mindful of all the ways spirit shows up and moves. We had no idea what would happen, but we knew that coming together would enliven our faith as Black UUs.

So, with revival in mind, the worship team set out to cocreate worship spaces each day of the gathering that would capture 1) what BLUU values most in worship; 2) how we hold people in our worship spaces; and 3) where we hoped to go in worship as a community. And each of these has informed every service we've led: before revival, during revival, and since.

What BLUU values most in worship

Any meaningful conversation about what BLUU values in worship must begin with the question: what are we worshipping, anyway? Quite simply, we worship the holy. That thing that unites us and the energy or spirit that binds us. We worship that which arrives to call us into a deeper relationship with and care for one another, the spirit of life that arises in community and that cannot be fully explained in words or contained in any single tradition. And while some may call that thing God, or Goddess, or Spirit, many others use many other names, and some don't call it anything at all. So our entry point is that we all get to show up whole, with whatever we bring that invites all of us into deeper connection to our own and other people's humanity or faith. Theological diversity is not just a catchy phrase; it is an unflinching lived experience and experiment.

Showing up whole also means centering our Blackness in our Unitarian Universalism. Because so much of who we are and what we've contributed to this faith has been shoved aside in UU congregations, we are very clear that, in order to settle comfortably into BLUU worship (whether online or in person), you have to open yourself up to an articulation of Unitarian Universalism that is unapologetically Black, created and developed by Black folks. This is the main reason why, when the revival worship team was considering what would go on our altar at the front of the room, we had a lengthy discussion about whether Black folks might feel more connected to a ritual of pouring libations from a pitcher than to one of lighting a chalice. We ended up doing both, but the conversation was meaningful and necessary.

And finally, being Black, without the emotional and spiritual impediments of the white gaze and the proscriptions of white supremacy culture, we give ourselves permission in worship to take up space and to take our time. Hence my response to the question that dear person asked. We were far less concerned about how long we might sit in worship together than about people getting their needs met and their spirits fed while we were together. However much time that would take. We knew that people would need different things and would take different amounts of time to get what they needed in that worshipful space, and that was fine. With options and opportunities to engage differently, we knew that many more people would leave satisfied and ready for more.

How we hold one another in worship

Since the very first BLUU worship services I helped plan (at BLUU's Convening) and participated in (at General Assembly), both in New Orleans in 2017, it has been clear that part of how we hold one another in the space of worship is by and through our Black cultural experiences and references. I remember planning worship for the BLUU Convening, which was the first time BLUU brought together Black folks from across Unitarian Universalism to build community and assess need, and geeking out over the jazz funeral theme that would be used for one of the services at that gathering. When I was planning BLUU's GA worship service with Rev. Amanda Weatherspoon, now the associate minister at River Road Unitarian Universalist Congregation in Bethesda, Maryland, we thought it more than appropriate to offer "Wake Up Everybody," by Harold Melvin and the Blue Notes (1975), as our opening song, and the joy people felt, and their connection to worship in that moment, was incredible to witness. We did not hand out lyrics, but most everybody knew them! And the ones who didn't were just as grateful to experience what was happening.

What many of us have clearly articulated is a need for a Black Unitarian Universalism that offers an unequivocal and unwavering sense of home to Black people who feel held by, or want to be more connected to, Black ancestry, Black love, Black thought, Black artistry, and Black faith. What we want is a Unitarian Universalism that, at every turn, honors, uplifts, and equips our Black lives.

Where we hope to go in worship

We always endeavor to go deeper into a worshipful experience that is not bound by time or space. And so at the revival we took our time, as we prepared for that Saturday evening service, to reimagine what a worshipful moment could be like if everyone were able to get their needs met. In the end, the service had stunning music, and I give thanks to David B. Smith, Executive Director of Worship at All Souls Tulsa, for that. We were blessed with powerful and impactful preaching, and I give thanks to Bishop Yvette Flunder, founder of City of Refuge United Church of Christ and former Trustee on the Board of Starr King School for the Ministry, for that. The worship team, who I will be indebted to for the rest of my days, prepared five stations around the room for people to receive blessings as they needed them — one for water blessings, one where people could be anointed with oil, one with an altar for meditation and reflection, one for communion, and one for prayer in all the ways people pray.

There are no words to adequately describe what happened to us that evening. Worship started at 6:45 p.m. The music was stirring, and the preaching reminded us of our power and presence as Black people in Unitarian Universalism and in the world. From the moment the stations were opened, people were lined up at all of them, all over the sanctuary, and moving ever so gracefully from one to another. I remember how my whole self was engaged as I watched someone receive a water blessing, then go to the altar for silent reflection, and then turn the corner and come back up the aisle to me for communion and prayer. He left me in tears, shaking his head in amazement that, as a UU in *that* space, he was able to receive and receive and receive. He said later that he had never been so filled up in his life. And I know he wasn't the only one.

And the best part of it all? When the last song on the order of service ended at 9:30 p.m., nobody moved. Nobody! There was silence in that medium-sized room that was filled to the brim with people. You could hear a pin drop — because nobody, we quickly understood, was ready to be done with what they were experiencing. And so, from the back of that room, I managed to mouth to Minister David to keep singing. And so he did, and so too did the people gathered. The last notes were sung by the whole gathering at 10:30 p.m. that night. And then some folks started talking among themselves, and others gathered around the piano and sang more.

The 2018 revival changed us in the best possible ways. We were able to join with Black folks from all over the country for rest and renewal, for community building and connection. And we were able to catch a glimpse of what was possible when we put aside enough of what we've been told and taught about Unitarian Universalism to really live into it more, and with our Blackness as the primary organizing principle through which to understand both it and ourselves better.

Leaving that space was difficult. In it folks were able to grow simultaneously in their Unitarian Universalism and their Blackness, and they didn't want to return to what they'd grown accustomed to back home. Folks didn't want to leave their Blackness at the door anymore, to fear showing up as their whole selves. Folks wanted the music that gave them life. Folks wanted to be together, learning and growing in community. I had more pastoral care calls in the two months after revival than I had ever had before or since, because folks were grieving the loss of that experience. And the leadership of BLUU knew, with a clarity of vision that only a revival could bring, that the development of BLUU Havens and BLUU Harbors (Black UU social groups and spiritual communities, respectively) and a deeper understanding of what a Black Unitarian Universalist worldview is, could be meaningful responses to that grief.

Because it was such a defining moment for our BLUU spiritual family and set such a powerful tone for the work that was before us, I have talked about the brilliance of that service on more than one occasion. When I mentioned it during a recent panel discussion, someone suggested that it made sense that Black folks would want to stay in worship for nearly four hours. But I quickly suggested that they not chalk that Saturday evening service up to us just being Black. I think the lesson to take from that evening is that people, everyday people, were so joyful about what they were receiving in their bodies, their minds, their hearts, and their spirits that they wanted more of it. They wanted so much more of it that they refused to get up when the last song had clearly been sung.

How would congregational rules, official or unofficial, about the length of worship shift if folks loved the experience so much that they could not help but stay for more? That's a question worth discussing.

What is missing from worship in your community that would allow bodies, minds, hearts, and spirits to fully engage and belong?

Ecstasy in Arab Musical Spaces

Rev. Summer Albayati

> *How does the music in your congregation engage you spiritually?*

Some might say that music is poetry in motion because it creates a physical response that gets our bodies to move or dance, within or without. Perhaps it is because it taps into emotions we were unaware of, like a poem that describes a place within our soul that we did not know existed.

There's a poem by Jalal ad-Din Mohammad Rumi that implores us to dance in ecstasy. It reminds us that we are all a part of God and even dust dances in this light, in celebration. But how many of us realize that the Sufi Islamic poetry of Kabir, Hafiz, and Rumi, poetry we may have used in worship, may not be translated well—that Islamic theology has been omitted from those translations? How many of us understand that these poems speak, not just of love, but of unity with the divine, and that they embody what that unity represents? Perhaps some of us wonder how the Sufi Islamic poets know what we have always longed for—love. The poets may express our longings, but I have found that our worship services can sometimes keep us from embracing those desires. Sometimes it feels as if we almost get there, but then we stop. It is as if we are afraid to go too deep—to immerse ourselves in the breathtaking moments of love—to dance, to dance.

As a Muslim Unitarian Universalist, I have been looked at with disdain when I have brought, to a UU worship space, a part of my Islamic culture that was not socially acceptable, such as by clapping or calling out. These vocal and physical responses to the worship experience were outward expressions of my inward journey toward ecstasy as I interacted with those facilitating the worship. They seemed, however, to make some around me uncomfortable, so I learned to suppress them.

As an Arab Muslim musician, I have had and facilitated transformative ecstatic experiences within spaces made sacred by music. The music that Arabs refer to as "classical" can emulate the emotional journey toward ecstasy that Sufi Muslims make in rituals such as dancing (as the whirling dervishes do) and rhythmic chanting (*dhikr*). By moving their bodies, and with the help of voices, drums, flutes, and other instruments, they enter into a trance. In its ideal form, the music takes both its performers and its listeners through a series of emotive responses that end in the mode of consciousness known as ecstasy. This musical ecstasy is called *tarab*.

Tarab reflects the Islamic culture of which it is a part and thus focuses on transforming hearts. Islam recognizes that the heart is born pure and good, but life experiences within our families, communities, and societies shape and change us. Thus we need reminders of the divine, and tools to help us connect with the divine spirit, in order to heal and transform our hearts and communities.

I can only describe the experience of *tarab* in terms of how you might feel during and after an extraordinary concert by one of your favorite bands. This musical journey will take you to a feeling of ecstasy, possibly with tears and laughter along the way, thus facilitating a healing, a softening—a transformation within your heart. Our congregational worship experience will ideally do the same—but are we ready to regularly facilitate such liberative experiences that allow an ecstatic response?

In the Arabic musical space, it is not uncommon for moments of ecstasy to be apparent when the audience responds to and participates in the music. People may clap, whistle, or yell; ululate, give long sighing cries, or call out "Allah." The musicians also respond to the singer by emulating the vocalizations upon their instruments. These responses are like the call and response found in a Black preaching style, which also involves responses from the congregants, or in the musical exchange between jazz musicians who are improvising on stage. There is an ecstatic feeling associated with creating something so real and authentic and unplanned. Musicians and audience members exchange energies in the performance, cocreating the experience in real time, and the musicians may adjust their playing to fit the needs of the other participants. When this is all done well, the listeners and musicians feel transformed; they are taken to another state, and afterward they may be left wondering what just happened. Time appears to stop.

It is that feeling that time has stopped that I call a trance, and it was something I experienced on a regular basis as I played Arabic music for many hours. The musical journey I took as a performer, connecting with the audience and other musicians, sensing their needs as well as my own, was transformative, leaving me with a feeling of ecstasy by the end of the evening. No concert experience was the same. All participants—musicians and audience—cocreated and facilitated the experience of *tarab* or ecstasy.

In this state, I noticed that my feelings of compassion, mercy, and love toward people were heightened. I believe that *tarab* can help heal the trauma we experience as participants in white supremacy culture within our congregations. I have often wondered if our congregations would benefit from regularly making such an emotional journey—making a focused effort to create, receive, and react to the emotions evoked within worship, not running away from the experience but leaning into it even more. Certainly, there are songs that we sing each week that make us feel sad or happy. There are songs that the choir sings that tell a story that taps into our emotions. There are songs that give us courage or make us angry because the words remind us of our childhood pains. There are songs that make us feel elated and want to rise. But can we sustain that feeling, or must we experience it only in that moment or even let it pass us by, stifling our feelings and our reactions, making ourselves unemotional because too much emotion is not socially acceptable?

I recognize that some may fear the term *ecstasy*. This word may evoke images of hysteria or out-of-control behaviors, but that is certainly not what I have experienced in Arabic musical spaces. Our society and, thus, our congregations reflect a culture that was created hundreds of years ago within a racist and colonialist ideology that sought to control the behaviors of the Indigenous peoples, the Africans who were brought here and enslaved, and other members of its society. What if we were to examine our Unitarian Universalist culture and let parts steeped in white supremacy go? What if we were to experience what some other cultures embrace, by using the musical journey to tap into our emotions? What if we allowed ourselves to move to the beats as we feel called, to clap, yell, free our voices more, and connect with the worship leaders on a level we would not normally find on a Sunday morning?

What if we were to let go of the white supremacy cultural attributes of perfection and control and allow worshippers to cocreate the sacred journey in real time? What might happen? Perhaps, if we did this, we would facilitate a healing that sets us on a path to ecstatic and transformative love—a path toward true justice, as we learn to embrace more compassion, show more mercy, and embody a love greater than we ever imagined. I wonder, are we truly ready to provide such radical hospitality in our sacred spaces, or will our colonial forebears continue to dictate our future?

If we truly want to become the multicultural denomination that welcomes and celebrates all, creating the beloved community and sending love into the world, should we consider using the Arabic musical journey and *tarab* as tools to liberate us on our path? Are we truly ready to embrace the ecstatic experience, or will we remain frozen in time—static—clinging to a way of being that does not value emotive responses to an inner longing? If love truly is the answer, isn't it time we found more love? Perhaps the answer is to open our hearts to the ecstatic celebration that Rumi calls us to in his poem.

Beloveds, now is the time to join in the ecstatic dance of the universe. Now is the time to embrace liberation. If not now, then when?

Why might your congregation engage more fully in music that embraces the kinds of cultural and emotional responses Rev. Summer Albayati describes?

A Conscious Act to Stay Engaged

Dr. Jenice L. View

What keeps you in Unitarian Universalism?

As a third-generation native Washingtonian, I am used to
DC's influx and outflow of people seeking higher education,
political fame and fortune, or professional validation at the
national level. My people were poor and working-class participants in the Great Migration, so we had a less starry-eyed
view of the city than did others. Similarly, my experience of
the Unitarian Universalist faith, and of All Souls Church Unitarian—"the prophetic voice of Unitarian Universalism in the
nation's capital"—has been moderated by a different vision of
what church and faith are called to do for the world.

I am a lifelong Unitarian Universalist, my mother having joined All Souls in 1959 when I was a year old and
she was a college student at Howard University, married
to an erstwhile member of the Nation of Islam. Nearly all
of my religious education, including About Your Sexu-
ality (the precursor to Our Whole Lives), was framed by
Unitarian Universalist theology. My marriage in 1984 to a
formerly unchurched Jamaican British immigrant and the
religious education of our two children, a nephew, and two
nieces were all informed by a welcoming faith that grappled with the social justice issues of our day—the sanctuary

movement, feminism, LGBTQ inclusion, the antiapartheid movement, environmentalism, war, climate change, and more. I am culturally Black, and therefore familiar with my maternal grandmother's and aunt's Baptist churches, and a great lover of Black gospel music. Still, each time Unitarian Universalist people proved to be flawed humans steeped in white supremacy culture, I nevertheless returned to UU theology.

A sign of stupidity? Inertia? Masochism? Internalized oppression? No, a conscious act of discernment and faith.

White supremacy culture in the land of Unitarian Universalists

While there is no scientific support for the idea that there are different "races" among humans, there is ample evidence of the social belief in "race" as a descriptor of people. In the United States, people who are defined as "white" are positioned as the dominant political and economic actors.

All of U.S. culture is steeped in white supremacy culture — hard stop. That statement needs no elaboration, given the history of Indigenous genocide, African enslavement, Mexican land theft, imperialism in Alaska and the Caribbean and the South Pacific, lynchings, legal racial segregation, persistent socioeconomic and political inequities, government violence against Indigenous peoples, Blacks, Latinx, and Asian people, and so on.

In their 2001 workbook, *Dismantling Racism,* Kenneth Jones and Tema Okun list some of the characteristics of white supremacy culture that work to maintain and promote the social, political, and economic dominance of "white" people:

perfectionism; a sense of urgency; defensiveness; an emphasis on quantity over quality; a worship of the written word; paternalism; either/or thinking; power hoarding; a fear of open conflict; individualism; a definition of progress that emphasizes being bigger and more; belief in objectivity; and insistence on a right to comfort.

Most churches in the U.S. that are rooted in Jewish and Christian theologies have been complicit in perpetuating white supremacy culture, beginning with religious justifications for the aforementioned atrocities and oppressions. Black churches—particularly those that subscribe to the social gospel, such as the African Methodist Episcopal Church—believe in equal rights, self-defense against racial violence, racial pride, and economic opportunity for Black Americans. The Black social gospel influenced ministers such as Rev. A. D. Williams and Revs. Martin Luther King Jr. and Sr. Yet many twentieth-century Black churches, including the more conservative Baptist churches, believed that suffering on earth would be rewarded in heaven.

My mother, who grew up Baptist, was introduced to Unitarian Universalism when a Howard University professor mentioned an unusual local church that vocally opposed anti-Asian sentiment during the Korean War and resisted the racial segregation of the police-organized Boys' Club by ejecting it from the church's basement and forming its own racially integrated after school program. Agnostic or atheist that she was, she nonetheless discovered a theology that suited her need for a welcoming faith community. The setting for my early religious education was thus determined.

At All Souls, we are all of us. We are all ages, all genders, all sexual orientations; all kinds of Indigenous, and of Black

(Ugandan, Jamaican, Haitian, U.S.-born, etc.), and of Brown (Puerto Rican, Mexican, Cuban, South American, etc.), and of Asian (South Asian, Vietnamese, Chinese, Japanese, etc.), and of white (South African, British, U.S.-born, etc.). We are Jewish, and Muslim, and Christian, and atheist, and agnostic, and Pagan, and humanist, and not sure, and searching.

As we've tried to maintain our reputation as "that progressive church"—standing firm against public injustices, with a congregation that is more multicultural than most UU churches and fellowships—we have sometimes forgotten that the church is made up of people who attend for the reasons that most people attend church: to lay down our burdens, to enjoy one another's company, to celebrate our joys and grieve our sorrows. Most white people do not join simply to work for social change. Most people of color do not join for the privilege of sitting next to white people in the pews. In the years since 1959, All Souls has experienced several ugly, wrenching, and public episodes of racialized trauma. For all our professed exceptionalism, we are still flawed; in the words of a dear Black woman friend, "Unitarian Universalists are people, too."

When I have gotten angry with All Souls' failures to live up to its aspirations, when Beloved Community feels inadequate or fraudulent, I have sometimes retreated to the Black churches of my grandmother and aunt. When the nine Black congregants of Mother Emmanuel Church in Charleston, South Carolina, were murdered by a white supremacist on a Wednesday in 2015, my first impulse was to go to a Black church that Sunday. I could tolerate the references to the divinity of Jesus, and even the notion of Christian forgiveness, if it meant being allowed to wail, to sing through the pain, to be loudly and unapologetically Black and angry. But I was the chair of the All Souls Board of Trustees, the Black woman associate minister was scheduled to be in the pulpit, and rightfully she did not want to go it alone. She wanted a people's voices service, but my own need for healing conflicted with the church's need to "make sense" of the horror. I felt I had nothing useful to say, and really, *really* did not want to hear white liberals fretting. But I decided to come clean with my struggle, and to express my hope that one day my first impulse following an example of racist, misogynist, homophobic, or anti-immigrant violence would be to turn to All Souls. It felt like an authentic sentiment, and saying it out loud, during a church service, seemed like a step toward making my church such a place.

Until. A white woman said in the fellowship hall afterward, rather petulantly, "I am sorry that you do not feel we are working hard enough to make you feel welcome and held." I wanted to scream, "It is *not about you!*" First of all, despite her reputation as a super-volunteer, she was not the only person working hard at church. More importantly, she was not solely responsible for my spiritual growth and development, for "working hard enough," for making me feel welcome and held. I had chosen a faith, and by 2015 it was a choice that my husband and I reevaluated at the start of every church year. "Is this still our church?" we ask ourselves. Unitarian Universalism is a faith that allows congregants to choose our leadership and our governance structure; it is not imposed on us by any external body. We do not need social media, the Unitarian Universalist Association, or any other entity to tell us how to heal ourselves or to love one another.

Choosing to stay

So, like most Black UUs, I have kept attending the UU church for its theology. Jesus was a powerful and prophetic leader and one of the most important social activists in the history of humanity, as were the originators of all of the religions, social movements, and revolutions that have made flawed human structures more open, more loving, more equal. All Souls Church Unitarian has ratified the Eighth Principle, which affirms a journey toward spiritual wholeness by building Beloved Community and dismantling racism and other oppressions, and which acknowledges the many ways that Unitarian Universalism has contributed to oppression and the perpetuation of white supremacy culture. (For example, UUs were prominent in the American eugenics movement, as Rev. Mark Harris shows in his 2010 book, *Elite*.) I do not need to attend a church to live into the Eight Principles and the Six Sources. One of the beauties of choosing Unitarian Universalism is that I cannot be shamed into attending Sunday services. And there are Sundays when the prospect of encountering microaggressions at church, despite the uplifting sermon and music and hugs, feels like too much to deal with after a hard week of racism and misogyny both in my workplace and around the world.

But I am not a separatist. There is no all-Black world, and even if such a place existed, there would be flawed humans in it, too. Our spiritual challenge is to wrestle with the people in front of us: to figure out how to love and be loved, to secure justice for all, to feed everyone who is physically and spiritually hungry, and to nurture our children and youth and teach them the truth. I like having a place where I can sing, dance, cry, laugh out loud, debate, philosophize, be silent, learn, teach, question, and sometimes get answers, maybe even wisdom. Somehow church ends up being a convenient place to do all of this, in a community of others who are willing to dance, too.

How does your congregation actively nurture the spiritual growth and development of people of color?

Sparking the White Supremacy Teach-In

Aisha Hauser

If you are centered in your Unitarian Universalist community, what privilege do you experience? If you are not someone who is centered, what is your experience?

When Trayvon Martin and Tamir Rice were murdered, I felt an ache and sadness in my bones. Of course, there had been murders of Black and Brown people since Columbus landed in the Caribbean; however, there was something so deeply tragic about Black children being murdered with impunity by law enforcement and by a vigilante who was protected by the law during the time that this country had its first Black president in the Oval Office.

These tragedies compounded the centuries-long trauma inflicted on Black and Brown people. I knew that I had to be a part of finding some justice and transforming the cruel and broken system that continues to produce these unjust tragedies. I embraced the mandate to center the liberation of Black and Brown people, and most especially the liberation of Indigenous people and the descendants of enslaved Africans. This nation has never come to terms with its violent founding. Violent extractive capitalism has been central to all that has been created and built in it. When Black and Brown people are viewed and treated only as property or as a means to maintain oppressive systems, the result is an inherently unequal society—a society that will never have true justice or peace until the sins of the past are addressed and repaired.

Our Unitarian Universalist faith is not untarnished by the sins of this country. In fact, some of our congregations owe their wealth to industries, such as cotton, that relied on enslaved and exploited labor. What does that mean for how we decolonize our wealth? How do we begin the necessary conversations about making reparations to descendants of enslaved Africans and to the Indigenous people whose land we occupy?

As a result of the UU White Supremacy Teach-In movement, an estimated seven hundred congregations have begun to have these pointed and difficult conversations. The Teach-In movement was unprecedented in its scope, and it was just the beginning of a crucial engagement. These conversations have angered some and empowered others. They are, for the first time, honest conversations. What is at stake is the heart and soul of Unitarian Universalism. We are a people of faith, a faith that demands of us reflection, determination, and, yes, a commitment to justice. Centering the voices of the marginalized will be part of becoming whole as a faith and as a people.

The UU White Supremacy Teach-In movement began in March 2017, after the president of the UUA was asked difficult questions about the association's predominantly white leadership. It was after receiving a lackluster and unhelpful response that I vented my frustration to Kenny Wiley. When I said I wanted to write a letter to complain, he suggested posting on social media. I asked Christina Rivera, the person we would later find out was turned down for a leadership position, if she would be okay with my making noise on social media about a woman of color being turned down in favor of yet another white male, and she offered her support. The posts immediately went viral and Christina, Kenny, and I wanted to harness the energy that was clearly stirred up in our faith movement. We decided to invite congregations to disrupt business as usual and hold a UU White Supremacy Teach-In. About twenty-five leaders — mostly religious educators, but also ministers, musicians, and others — collaborated on creating the materials for the website, and Black Lives of Unitarian Universalism hosted the materials until a separate website could be created.

Many white UUs were confused by hearing the UUA described with the term "white supremacy culture." The teach-ins that congregations were invited to take part in were intended to help them understand and illustrate how no one in the United States is separate from the oppressive systems that have shaped the dominant culture's narratives and norms.

Since that spring, I have traveled the country preaching and offering workshops to congregations and secular groups. One question I've encountered several times is "What do we do if we are all white?" It is usually asked by a minister or congregational leader who is committed to antiracism and antioppression work but doesn't know where to start.

My response is always the same: "White space is not neutral. If you are in an all-white space, find out how it got that way." What laws were passed to keep Black families from buying or renting homes in your area? What genocide might have taken place to "clear" the land for settlers? What laws are still maintained to keep your setting from becoming integrated? Focusing on the history of place is one way to engage with our responsibilities as benefactors of generations of policies that centered the needs of people of European descent.

Some UUs have resisted the teach-in movement. But most have accepted it as one way to learn about oppressive systems in order to transform them into more just ones. Some UUs have argued that the use of the term "white supremacy culture" is inappropriate, because—they say—it is a false claim about our liberal faith. They resist seeing the ways in which white supremacy is woven through and manifested in Unitarian Universalism because they don't want to think of themselves as implicated in maintaining and benefiting from it; they are more comfortable admitting that individual UUs may, unfortunately and occasionally, commit racist acts than that UU culture is white supremacist. But the work of dismantling systems of oppression and creating a more just world must not be hindered by a requirement to use only language that those who benefit from the current systems are comfortable with. As the writer and activist Ijeoma Oluo says, "If you are comfortable when talking about race, you are doing it wrong."

Faith communities are where humans learn what it means to exist with each other and for a higher purpose, whether or not that purpose is a promised afterlife. At times, Unitarian Universalists have answered the call to justice with honor, such as in the fight for marriage equality and when UU ministers followed Rev. Dr. Martin Luther King's call to go to Selma. At other times, our faith has missed the mark. Some of the most tragic examples include the embrace by some Unitarians of the early twentieth-century eugenics movement, the rejection of Rev. Ethelred Brown's request to start a Black Unitarian Church in Harlem in 1920, and the white-led General Assembly failure, in 1968, to deliver on a financial promise made to the Black Unitarian Caucus. That failure prompted hundreds of Black Unitarians to leave the faith, the majority never to return.

Time cannot be turned back. What we can do is learn from the past and make every effort to not repeat our mistakes and injustices.

An experience of Unitarian Universalism absent the dominant culture

In mid-March of 2017, I was in New Orleans, on the top floor of the DoubleTree Hotel, in a room full of Black UUs and Black UU–adjacent folks. I had been hired by the organizers of Black Lives of Unitarian Universalism (BLUU) to co-lead the youth programming, along with Kenny Wiley and Kimberly Quinn Johnson, at BLUU's first Convening. It hit me, as we were gathered, that I was feeling a deep joy and contentment that I had never felt in UU spaces before. I realized that this was because the UUism I was experiencing wasn't centering any of the transcendentalists, or any white person, past or present. The joy came from the centering of Black community. The organizers of BLUU had been clear from the start that the journey was going to be messy, and it would be one we took together.

During the Convening, I experienced sacred space that was rooted in liberation and love of Black people. I was inspired to read more Black writers, including James H. Cone, who has written extensively about Black liberation theology.

His 2011 book, *The Cross and the Lynching Tree*, took him ten years to write, and in working on it he grappled with the knowledge that he or anyone in his family could have been a victim of this horrific crime.

As I've become more and more immersed in the ideas of liberation theology, I have found them more and more central to my faith and to how I live my life. I have not taken the invitation to be a part of the BLUU community for granted. I am not a descendant of enslaved Africans. I am an immigrant, born in Egypt, with great-grandmothers from both Europe and Sudan. Like other recent immigrants of the African diaspora, I live with the experiences of racism, xenophobia, and othering.

I had another opportunity to experience Black-centered UUism at the Harper-Jordan Symposium, sponsored by BLUU in the fall of 2019. The event was attended mostly by BIPOC people (Black, Indigenous, and People of Color); white people were in the minority. It's hard for me to put the experience into words. It was the most sacred Unitarian Universalist space I've ever been a part of. I was invited to speak on one of the six exclusively Black panels, and it was an honor and privilege. Instead of offering prepared texts, the panelists responded to questions from the panel moderator, Dr. Takiyah Amin; the format was designed to ensure that we answered in the moment, with whatever her questions prompted in us. I spoke about my experience as a UU who had brought with me into UUism my experience of the Muslim faith.

I was also struck by the strong presence and centering of the Black queer experience throughout the symposium. Many of the panels had at least one person from the LGBTQ community, often more. It is not often that Black-centered faith communities embrace and celebrate the fullness and holiness of the Black LGBTQ experience.

Unitarian Universalism's potential to fully embrace and authentically include BIPOC LGBTQ community members is immense, and it shouldn't be taken lightly or squandered. Unitarian Universalism should offer love, affirmation, and inclusion to people who have been rejected as a matter of course, unhesitatingly, rather than an intellectual exercise.

After the symposium, I co-led a program for UU ministers at which everyone, except for me, was white. I asked the only other person who had attended the symposium to tell the group about her experience. She said, "I felt more UU there than I did in my entire life, and I have to think about what that means."

What she said surprised me, warmed my heart, and affirmed for me what the BIPOC community has been naming and lifting up: that centering the voices of Black UUs creates a richer and holier experience for everyone.

The more Unitarian Universalism affirms and encourages people in the fullness of who they are and how they show up, the more, and the more deeply, they will engage with it. Centering the experiences of people with marginalized identities will enrich the UU faith.

How will you center people with marginalized identities in your Unitarian Universalist community?

Leading Equitable Multicultural Communities

Dr. Janice Marie Johnson

Why do you yearn for (in the words of Dr. Mark Hicks) a "multiracial, multicultural, theologically and generationally diverse spiritual community?"

I write these words from my home office in Brooklyn. I do not play background music; rather, I listen to the sirens of ambulances as they rush from one place to another, aiming to save lives. My neighborhood is usually quiet, very quiet. I live between two worlds, one Chinese-American, the other Hasidic. I am a Black internationalist who lives at the nexus of my Unitarian Universalist faith and that of others, my Caribbean ethnicity and that of others, my Jamaican culture and that of others, my religion and that of others.

As the COVID-19 virus maintains its stranglehold on the world, I wonder if my contribution to this book will have any value in a UU context. I wonder if it will have any relevance in a UU future.

I have to believe that it does . . . that it will . . . that it must. Soul searching is not at all new to me. It begins, subtly, when as a committed Unitarian Universalist I start to notice myself questioning my place within the Unitarian Universalist community.

I do so as a Black woman, a woman of color communing within a denomination that has an overwhelmingly white membership. It is at times daunting, at times annoying, and at times beyond frustrating.

And I know, as I know my own face, body, and sensibility, that this is my faith. I want multiculturalism to be central to this faith. I want this faith to be so strong that it is unshakeable throughout the United States of America and throughout the world: in Tokyo, Japan; in Kampala, Uganda; in Oaxaca, Mexico; in Manila, in the Philippines; in the Khasi Hills of India; and everywhere.

Without question, I know that I deserve a place at the UU table. I also know that each of us deserves this privilege. I recognize my longing for multicultural connection within this faith that I cherish. Years ago, I wanted to be warmly welcomed into our congregations. I still have that desire, but nowadays I want more. I want each of us to belong to an equitable congregation. I want multicultural leadership, music, worship, and governance to be woven into the fabric of our congregations.

In these especially tenuous times, I find myself wondering to what degree members of our congregations are aware of the urgent need, as I am. In my heart of hearts, I know that fighting for equity will transform our lives, deepen our faith, and enrich our souls as we build and experience community in new ways.

In order for this transformation to begin, each of us must be intentional about reaching toward Beloved Community. We must do so fiercely. We all must be clear about what we are willing to give up. This will not happen without each person knowing what's at stake for us as individuals. Our congregations deserve no less, whether people of color are members of them or not.

I used to work to create multicultural sensibility. Now I'm fighting for a racial equity that honors the essence of multiculturalism. I no longer have interest in or yearning for "the browning of the pews."

In order to build Beloved Community, Unitarian Universalist congregations need to expand the welcome table and commit to decentering whiteness. This is simultaneously uncomplicated and difficult. Leaders and congregants alike must dig deeply into their souls. They must look at their reflections in the mirror as they ask themselves, "What must I give up in order to build this community? Why must I give it up?"

Although it is not easy to move from a sense of "unknowing" to a sense of "knowing," this is what is required of us. We are blessed to have access to books and other high-quality resources that can teach us about relationship and help us on our journey, but we need more. Giving money to BLUU, DRUUMM, and other BIPOC-led UU organizations is a good start, but a better one is engaging with the people who drive the organizations and make them thrive. We need to engage with those we think of as "the other." We need a reverence for the relational.

When the stakes are high, each of us must be ready to answer "Yes." This is what that precious hymn "Just as Long as I Have Breath," #6 in *Singing the Living Tradition*, reminds me of. It reminds me to ever answer "Yes" to life. "Yes" to Love. "Yes" to truth. What we can gain from answering "Yes" is greater than anything that we might imagine.

In answering "Yes," I, too, must give something up. I must give up on my own lack of faith and my apathy about who we might be and who we might become.

Among the Zulu-speaking tribes of northern Natal in South Africa, the most common greeting, equivalent to "hello" in English, is the expression *sawubona*. It means "I see you." If you are a member of the tribe, you might reply by saying *sikhona*, "I am here." The order of the exchange is important: until you see me, it implies, I do not exist. This implication is part of the spirit of *ubuntu*, a frame of mind prevalent among the peoples of sub-Saharan Africa. The Zulu saying *Umuntu ngumuntu ngabantu* means "A person is a person because of other people." This frame of mind brings richness into our communications and conversations, our discoveries, and the articulations of our dreams.

It is imperative that we as a denomination transform how we relate across racial, ethnic, and cultural differences. The mission priorities of the UUA are to

- equip congregations for healthy and vital ministry,
- train leaders with credentialing and support for ministry in our time, and
- amplify UU values in the public sphere, nationally and globally.

In order to meet those priorities, our congregations and communities must disrupt the workings of racism. They must move vigilantly toward equitable relational space. This movement starts when we truly "see" and "hear" each other into existence. As faith-filled people, we need as many sacred moments as we can find. The late Rev. Marjorie Bowens-Wheatley reminded us that the community we belong to is all of life. In those grace-filled moments of greeting, we know we're all a part of the relational.

When my daughter Lehna was a little girl, I took her to one of my favorite spots, the Whitney Museum in New York City. I could hardly believe that at her tender age, she asked me, "Mom, why are these African masks owned by white people?" What a rude awakening. . . . I wondered how best to respond. I asked myself, "What are the nursery rhymes and campfire songs for young ones of color?"

Several years later, she observed, "When I was little, people thought I was cute; now, no one at church knows what to say to me. . . ." I tell her that there's the intersection of age and race. How I wish that we adults would take the time to learn how to speak with our children, youth, and young adults.

Cultural competence demands that we first know who we are, then learn who others are. It requires of us a holy curiosity about, and a willingness to embrace, other ways of being. It requires us to understand a landscape far larger than the parochial one in which we were raised, whatever it was! It requires of us a deep cultural humility that calls us to decenter ourselves as we center the gifts of whoever is in our midst.

I am not convinced that we are ready to make this bold move forward.

I ask myself, as I ask you, "How can we empower and support Unitarian Universalist individuals and congregations in building the multicultural Beloved Community we boldly say we want to embody?"

Let me suggest that we do so deliberately, with intention. We do so with a firm commitment to making the structural changes required to embrace, in this twenty-first century, a Unitarian Universalism that is fierce, spirit-filled, and generous enough to be true to many—perhaps even all.

Living into this commitment will not be comfortable, but it is necessary for us to truly build the world we dream about, engaging in beloved conversations of depth, heart, and commitment.

Let us be mosaic makers, as Rev. Alicia Forde calls us to be in her poem in Kathleen Montgomery's edited collection *Bless the Imperfect:* "practitioners of justice, / called to respond to brokenness in the world," piecing the broken bits together.

We are blessed to live in a time, a new time, when we can develop our antiracist, antioppressive, and multicultural habits and skills in order to prepare ourselves to nurture a multiculturally competent, actively antiracist congregation.

Digging deeply into our roots, we can learn our true identities and stories. We can claim our part in our respective pasts . . . and learn far more about colonialism than we were ever taught. We can take an unflinching look at empire. We can teach ourselves and each other that terms such as "antiracist," "white supremacy," and "Indigenous" are not dirty words. We can acknowledge that white supremacy has an insidious ability to shape even our faith-filled lives.

Just as long as we have breath, let us act for justice, for faith, and for the realization of Beloved Community.

As I listen to the sirens surrounding me, ever reminding me that tomorrow is not promised to me, to mine, or to anyone anywhere, I reaffirm my commitment to a negation of empire, of colonialism, of white supremacy, and of all that would make any of us "less than."

I know that the international, national, and local death tolls are terrible. I also know that my people—people of color—will succumb to COVID-19 at far greater rates than others in this country.

I want us, as UUs, to recognize the moment in which we find ourselves. We were there for Stonewall. We were there for Selma. We were there for Ferguson. We were there for Standing Rock. We were there for the Dakota Access Pipeline. We were there for Sanctuary. We were there for immigration rights . . . decarceration . . . bail. . . .

Let us fiercely commit ourselves to a bold justice that ensures that Black and Brown people, including those who care for our sanctuaries, are treated with the same respect given to white people. Let us also commit ourselves to fighting internalized racism, which can tear families apart. Historically, some Black as well as white people privileged light-skinned Blacks (notoriously, those who passed the "brown paper bag test") over their dark-skinned siblings. In addition to prejudice against darker-skinned persons, modern shadism or colorism is linked to prejudice on the basis of non-Eurocentric speech patterns, manners, body language, or convictions. All these divide us.

Let us commit to living every moment in a faith-filled presence, one that nourishes us as Unitarian Universalists committed to, in the words of the hymn, "all that is our life." There you have it: my multilayered, multifaceted understanding of and commitment to multiculturalism within a UU context. May it be so.

What are the next steps toward making your community "multiracial, multicultural, theologically and generationally diverse"?

Nurturing Mission-Based Arts Programs

Laura Weiss

Who are the leaders in your arts community?

Spirituality is expressed through the arts. We are often moved when listening to a choir, gazing at a colorful abstract painting, or observing the grace of a dancer. Artistic expression is the relational gift that connects the divinity within each of us to that within others. Being a creator or participant within the expressive arts community allows us to encounter deeply the holy within all, drawing us closer to building Beloved Community. We experience company in the darkness that emerges and find beauty in unexpected places. Our full engagement in spiritual life should include engaging with art in order to deepen our understanding and witness. The arts can be a conduit to healing, giving space to speak what otherwise could not be spoken. Allowing for ancestral pain and pride to find a vehicle for communication, in time cultivating communal healing and hope, shared artistic mediums hold our spirits as we journey through difficult paths.

At the Unitarian Universalist Congregation of Fairfax, Virginia, we seek to expand the spiritual lives of our congregants and build a more beloved community through a broad definition of the arts. We have empowered a multidisciplinary volunteer team to encourage more of us to engage in and spread the spiritual experience of artistic work. We have not only engaged in the important work of identifying artistic leadership; we are striving to broaden that leadership and lean into multidisciplinary and multigenerational artistic spiritual *community*. It is very exciting artistic ministry.

People can experience the holy through many artistic mediums. We often assume that people want to hear music in our worship and congregational life; yet arts programs in spiritual communities must go beyond that single medium. A team of varied professional leaders can reach members who are drawn to a wider variety of artistic forms and spiritual access points and match more of them to their interests or strengths.

At Fairfax, we have chartered a Music and Arts Team to examine how the artistic experience can promote the congregation's strategic goals and to conceptualize and implement multidisciplinary, multiage artistic programs and productions that support its mission. Team members recruit artistic leaders of all ages to engage deeply with the mission, not just to perform. Leaders are encouraged to broaden their spiritual practice through a lens of building artistic community. An example might include inviting artists with strong leadership potential o help lead a beginners' group in collaboration with the Music and Arts Team. This not only enriches the spiritual life of the lay leader but also promotes ever-expanding circles of artistic ministry. Because the program is no longer centered on a single director, the lay leaders become seekers and builders of the community's vision.

All of our congregants and future congregants would grow in artistic spaces if we promote deeper soul healing, and if we work to cultivate leaders who themselves become connectors, there will be more ripples in the spiritual pond. Both artists and nonartists must be given opportunities for engagement in the ways that move them. The more people who engage in the work to establish a covenantal artistic community, the more our congregations will embody the spiritual work of Unitarian Universalism. All programs—music, visual art, dance, theater, and more—are part of the whole; each provides ways to connect with the community, and none should be dominant over the others. The arts are an essential element of building a more beloved, multigenerational, multiracial community, in both relational work and infrastructure.

And, very importantly, we should involve youth in every decision. We are working to find ways to recognize youth and children as the creative core of congregational life and in crafting our vision of the future. Their involvement reminds us all that it is important to live out our commitment to systemic change by developing nonhierarchical, community-based arts programming. Their familiarity with Internet culture, media tools, and marketing systems gives them a valuable understanding of our future and of organizational change. They are the emerging leaders in our faith. Enthusiastic youth and young adults can fuel everyone's engagement in congregational life by bringing forward vibrant and vital contributions.

To innovate in artistic programming within a congregation requires trust from the community. Deep listening and decentering can provide a foundation for building that trust, as can modeling vulnerability and curiosity. Including the arts in spiritual communities provides opportunities for nonverbal and emotional forms of understanding. To create an innovative arts experience such as this is difficult and often painful work, but it is also revolutionary and radical. When we shift to new ways of exploring the arts, we start to build a more authentic beloved relationship to one another.

Our work involves many voices. We work together to assess how we will live out our mission as Unitarian Universalists and as Fairfax community members through the arts. Our congregation is willing to boldly try new ideas and respond with grace even when we make mistakes and fail. For that we are grateful. Both our stumbles and our successes have been essential building blocks of this new programming direction, which we could not have established without community support. We have learned from our congregants that our program needs to be a space where all artistic mediums can coexist equally and where more voices can be heard than ever before. This is the work we feel has led to a deepening of our spiritual selves.

The ten members of Fairfax's Music and Arts team are all volunteers. They include two visual artists, two band leaders, two people responsible for programming jazz music, one each for choral, handbell, and children's music programming, and one person for theater. (Ten people may seem like a large group, but Fairfax is a mid- to large congregation. Notably, however, this model has worked in even the smallest congregations I have served over the past twenty years.)

The question this team asks again and again is not "What new thing can we build?" but rather "What already exists in our community, and how do we better connect to that divine spark? How are we becoming a more connected, engaged, multidisciplinary, multigenerational community that allows for meaningful spiritual engagement?" We often return to "How is this actually serving the mission?" It is crucial that the team represents so many different subsets of our congregation. Its members are like spokes radiating out from our central mission. They bring ideas, form partnerships, and work together. We have witnessed new engagement within our community from those who otherwise would not have encountered our UU church because team members invited them in to explore spiritual work through the arts. We see this as evidence that our program not only promotes the arts but also expands our Beloved Community and its footprint in the world. People with varied skills are stepping forward and reaching out, new bodies of artistic and collaborative material are being created, and artists and participants in the program are encouraging each other to reflect deeply on our work in the world.

The arts program at Fairfax is teaching us that Beloved Community blossoms and our relationships deepen through the arts when we explore multiple artistic disciplines, when we cultivate leaders, and when we decenter ourselves. We know that church communities must change in order to meet the needs of this new world and that centering younger, diverse, and often oppressed voices in artistic programs is a needed and important part of this change. For congregations to successfully cultivate artistic leadership, they must ensure from the start that that leadership of our programming represents a variety of ages and artistic mediums. Without decentering, we are unable to take the critical first step of learning where our programs reproduce white supremacy and working to uproot it. We have faith that this innovative approach to building artistic spiritual community is helping to engage people who would otherwise not be involved, and it has changed the way we interact.

By taking this approach, congregations can begin healing deep wounds. New artistic leaders are emerging from this work that will help shape the future of our community, our denomination, and the world.

How might the arts expand leadership in your community?

Social Class and Beloved Community

Denise Moorehead

When did you first become aware of class differences?

When I was five years old, I attended a birthday party for one of my friends and neighbors, a first-generation Italian American girl. We lived just two houses apart in a lower-middle-class—turning working-class—neighborhood. My friend had brothers and sisters, a working dad, and a stay-at-home mom. I was an only child with two working parents committed to providing me with every educational, social, and cultural advantage that had eluded them during their Depression-era segregated childhoods.

I woke up early the morning of the party and picked out a dress, patent leather shoes, and a matching handbag. My mother did my hair with ribbons. Together, Mom and I wrapped the birthday gift, and we headed two doors down to the party. There were games, snacks, and lots of giggling girls with a sprinkling of boys. I couldn't figure out why my friend was wearing pajamas to her own party, but I didn't say anything—at first. But when the time came to cut the birthday cake, I couldn't contain myself any longer. I said, "Aren't you ever going to put on your party clothes? The party will be over soon." She answered that she was in her new party clothes. I laughed, assuming that she was kidding, and blurted out,

"I have a nightgown just like that so I know that's not your new dress."

The girl turned red and was on the verge of tears. Her mother looked distraught, and my mom told me to apologize and then whisked me away before I could have cake. When I got home, she not only chastised me for being so thoughtless but spanked me. Later, she sat me down and explained that I had more than most of my neighbors because I was an only child. She did not, at the time, add that she and Dad had some college behind them, social connections through church and civic engagement, and community ties as third-generation residents of our city. While I did not know it at the time, this was my first awareness of class difference.

Over the next few years, I had many talks with my mom and dad about being aware of my relative privilege. I learned not to talk about my activities outside of the neighborhood— private summer camp, trips to places like the New York World's Fair, dance lessons at the best dance school in town, theater excursions, French camp, and more. I also learned not to talk about my neighborhood with my friends who lived elsewhere; they seemed bemused when I described my neighbors.

Four years after my birthday party faux pas our neighborhood became less safe. My family of three moved to a new area of the city, a solidly middle-class neighborhood. By then, my mother had left her factory job and now worked for the post office. My dad had been promoted to a higher rank in the Air Force. We had our own house, with a large yard, and my new local friends still did not have the same advantages I did.

As I grew older, I realized that my parents knew that I, as a Black female, would need these advantages. They worked hard to provide them, knowing they were necessary for a chance at a comfortable, fulfilling life. The children in my new neighborhood (all white except for us) would have certain advantages because of their race. They would not be subject to the systemic racism that, coupled with class limitations, could derail my life. This was my nascent understanding of what American lawyer, civil rights advocate, philosopher, and leading scholar of critical race theory Kimberlé Williams Crenshaw calls *intersectionality*. She developed the theory of intersectionality in 1989 to describe how overlapping or intersecting social identities, particularly minority identities, relate to systems and structures of oppression, domination, or discrimination.

So, technically, I'm a straddler: someone who moves to a more advantaged social class during their lifetime. As a straddler and a Black woman, I have a particular perspective on social class in the United States. But while I am technically a straddler, my parents' efforts to provide me with life's advantages give the term a slightly different meaning for me. As Black Americans who were born at the start of the Great Depression and who used every tool they had to fight white supremacy and classism, my parents knew that the most important class indicator they could give me was high expectations and aspirations. Therefore, I think of myself as a lower-middle-class child who enjoyed the best that a middle- and upper-middle-class life can offer.

This bifurcated class background made me aware of social class long before the Occupy Movement made class inequality a rallying cry. It also made me aware that even in post-Occupy America, most of us don't really understand how to define social class, nor can we tell you our class background or current class location. As Richard V. Reeves, Katherine Guyot, and Eleanor Krause discuss in a 2018 report for the Brookings Institution ("Defining the Middle Class: Cash, Credentials, or Culture?," www.brookings.edu/research/defining-the-middle-class-cash-credentials-or-culture), only about a tenth of Americans describe themselves as working class, and less than a twentieth as upper class. The vast majority of us place ourselves somewhere in the middle, almost regardless of our income.

Most Americans know that class differences can turn into divisive classism, keeping people from bringing their whole selves into relationships and causing misunderstandings and pain. At its worst, classism can stifle lives. Many Americans are unaware of the strengths with which their class background has imbued them and the positive ways it has shaped their worldview.

My class background as a straddler led me to devote my life to helping diverse communities bridge their differences and create Blessed Community. It eventually led me to the Unitarian Universalist Service Committee, where I worked for nearly ten years, with Unitarian Universalists and others, to advance justice and human rights globally. I was not a Unitarian Universalist when I arrived at the Service Committee, but I was when I left. How could I not be, when Unitarian Universalists were partnering with people halfway around the globe—people with whom they had little in common other than their belief in justice—to create a better world?

My work at the Service Committee brought me into contact with two women who would change my life. One was a Unitarian Universalist minister, the late Rev. Dorothy Emerson, and the other, Betsy Leondar-Wright, is an economic justice activist, sociologist, educator, and author—and, like me, a late convert to Unitarian Universalism. What began as a leisurely lunch together turned into a mission to help Unitarian Universalist congregations, organizations, and individuals break the silence about class in our lives. We began working together to transform our faith community. We countered the stereotypes and myths that justify unequal opportunity and worked to reduce classism in our faith community and make it more inclusive. We recognized that our progressive denomination had devoted significant resources over multiple decades to expanding diversity and inclusion in many areas at denominational, regional, and congregational levels. Yet there was still work to be done.

Unitarian Universalists have been leading religious voices for LGBTQ rights at the national level. We also have a long history of advocating for women's rights, and the Universalists were one of the first denominations in the United States to ordain a woman (Olympia Brown, in 1863). We have been on the front lines of the civil rights movement at the highest denominational levels and within the smallest societies, from the struggle against Jim Crow to the Black Lives Matter marches. We have supported the rights of disabled people. We've stood for workers' rights and against ethnic bias, which has been exacerbated in recent years by the radical right's attack on immigrants.

While the denomination's diversity focus has been both wide and deep, what we have not done in a sustained way until now is to explore class and classism with the same breadth and depth we have brought to other areas of bias. In fact, classism is often at the root of challenges that are misinterpreted as racism, gender bias, or another form of prejudice.

Together with my fellow class actionistas (a term coined by my friend, colleague, and mentor, Anne Phillips), and with support from the UU Funding Program, I founded UU Class Conversations. Our workshops, webinars, worship resources, videos, and more are based on our seven Unitarian Universalist Principles, especially the Third Principle: acceptance of one another and encouragement to spiritual growth in our congregations. Thanks to sustained support by the UU Funding Panel, the New York State Convention of Universalists, and Faithify supporters, this work has brought me into contact with congregations and organizations from Vermont to California and from New Mexico to Michigan. My colleagues and I have helped congregations examine their own class (and race) diversity and experiences and reflect on what class tells them—and all of us—about the appeal of the Unitarian Universalist message.

I have been heartened by my fellow Unitarian Universalists' hunger to share their class stories, even when they are painful. More than once I've had someone come up to me and whisper, "I'm passing. I'm not really middle class." And I have heard this from people with both relatively little and relatively great class advantage.

Just as people have a class background, organizations are perceived to have a class, and Unitarian Universalism is often assumed to be mostly middle to upper-middle class. A UU once told me that they had never finished their college degree, but they did not want their fellow congregation members to know. A man who owned a company that afforded him an annual income of two million dollars swore publicly that he was only upper-middle class. If you cannot feel comfortable sharing your class status with members of your congregation, how can you build true Beloved Community?

It is gratifying when people share, openly and honestly, about their class background and current class position in Class Conversations activities and trainings. I believe that this sharing is vital to strengthening our congregations and organizations, our social action work, and our ability to better welcome people with a wide range of class backgrounds.

Since 2013, UU Class Conversations, together with its partner organizations and many others in the denomination, has been able to raise the issues of class, classism, class privilege, class allyship, and the intersection of class and race in a provocative way. I was thrilled when the UUA Commission on Appraisal chose to study social class, issuing its report, *Class Action: The Struggle with Class in Unitarian Universalism*, in 2017. The Commission on Institutional Change examined the intersection of race and class in its 2020 report, *Widening the Circle of Concern*, which clearly lays out a pathway to achieve our shared mandate to "end systemic oppression in our Association."

As my late cofounder Rev. Dr. Dorothy Emerson often said, "This is indeed sacred work."

How can our Unitarian Universalist faith community build on class differences to become stronger and more welcoming?

Embracing Family Ministry

Laura Beth Brown

What is your childhood experience of worshipping as a family?

In southeast Texas, where I grew up, families are expected to attend church on Sundays. Although my parents had both been raised Christian, neither was churchgoing when I came along. My mother truly wanted to change that, but her demanding full-time job, coupled with primary responsibility for me, left her exhausted by Sunday. My father worked at an oil refinery with an equally grueling schedule that included overnight and weekend shifts in rotation, so church just wasn't happening for my family.

When I was five, my mother decided to reach out to the local Baptist church to ask if anyone from their neighborhood would be willing to drive me to and from church on Sundays. The congregation put her in touch with a retired couple who agreed to take on the responsibility of bringing me each Sunday. From kindergarten to third grade, I went to church almost every week with this older couple. I grew to trust and love several adults in that congregation, including, of course, the couple who committed to bringing me there.

By the time I had turned eight, my parents were having problems with their marriage. I convinced my mother to come to church with me. She began to make connections and find support there, and two years later, when my father got promoted and had more control of his work schedule, he joined us. In the end, my whole family found a loving and supportive community that inspired us to volunteer and share our talents. I grew up to be a leader in my youth group, my mother joined the choir, and my father found meaning in lay prison ministry.

I wonder where my parents would be if my mother had not asked for help. Or if she had felt she could not come to church because she was ashamed that her family was on the brink of falling apart. I wonder, also, where I would be if there had not been a village of people reaching out to support my parents so that my parents could support me. Taking a phrase from Reggie Joiner and Carey Nieuwhof's 2015 book, *Parenting Beyond Your Capacity*, I believe that that Southern Baptist faith family helped my parents parent beyond their capacity.

Faith communities have always been central to my life and have informed what I feel is central to my calling: helping people find and foster community. It is not surprising, therefore, that our Unitarian Universalist congregations' recent focus on family ministry has been a draw for me. Family ministry is what I have known and experienced in faith community at its best. It may take a variety of forms, such as whole-congregational worship, social action, and learning, but fostering multigenerational relationships is at the heart of them all. If families are not building supportive relationships in our congregations, they will find community elsewhere.

As the transitional director of lifespan faith development at the Unitarian Universalist Congregation of Binghamton, New York, Ann Kadlecek wrote that family ministry "seeks to meet people where they are and include families of all kinds—as families—in the life of the congregation. Family ministry is not just about families with children, but the family ministry model recognizes that families with children need significant attention" ("Family Ministry at UUCB: The Birth of the Binghamton Model," www.uua.org/files/pdf/f/family_min_binghamton_kadlecek.pdf). This final point cannot be overstated.

We know that parents are absolutely critical to the faith formation system. Work by the Pew Research Center has shown that parental involvement in children's religious education is the primary determinant of their continued engagement in their faith from their school years into adulthood ("One-in-Five U.S. Adults Were Raised in Interfaith Homes," www.pewforum.org/2016/10/26/links-between-childhood-religious-upbringing-and-current-religious-identity/). In other words, Unitarian Universalist parents are key to the faith's growth. Yet, as religious educator Kim Sweeney lifts up in her workshops, congregational religious education resources are most often funneled toward age-segregated Sunday morning programs, with little—if any—attention given to empowering parents in their role as primary religious educators. Why do we continue to do this?

Salsa, Soul, and Spirit: Leadership for a Multicultural Age, by Juana Bordas, gave me some insight. In this book, Bordas outlines what she calls a new social covenant that lifts up three principles: 1) *Sankofa*, the recognition that we must honor, respect, and examine the past in order to understand the present; 2) *I to We*, the movement from individualism to collective identity; and 3) *Mi Casa Es Su Casa*, a spirit of true generosity that holds collective cultures together.

Focusing on the second, Bordas explains that multicultural collectivist communities, or *we* cultures, have a "strong sense of belonging and sticking together," and "the family, community, or tribe takes precedence over the individual, whose identity flows from the collective." Collectivist communities also have "highly defined rules, and they change more slowly than individualist culture." *We* cultures "cherish group welfare, unity, and harmony," and because these communities are "tightly woven, there is a wholeness in which many things, including differences, can exist at once."

Although Bordas is speaking of multicultural communities, religious communities such as ours strive to live into these values. As Unitarian Universalist covenantal faith communities, we can be the antidote to the isolation families of all kinds experience in our individualist culture—which we now fully own as white supremacy culture, of which individualism is an aspect. Unfortunately, many people—having grown up in our white supremacy culture—simply do not know how to be in community.

It is important to recognize that we are not starting as multicultural collectivist communities of the kind that Bordas lifts up in her book, so the qualities inherent in those communities do not come naturally to us. I have described family ministry in my work as the white supremacy culture "buzzword" for collectivist community, to remind me of our history. For decades, Unitarian Universalists have emphasized the individual journey over the community experience. We will not be successful if we are not vigilant in breaking down this affinity for individualism and the many ways in which white supremacy manifests in our congregations.

White supremacy shows up when families are ashamed to ask for help, so they remain isolated. White supremacy shows up when families are embarrassed because they don't look like the family shown in a stock photo in a Hallmark picture frame. White supremacy shows up when parents prefer to pay others to engage their children rather than volunteering in their faith communities and owning their roles as their children's primary religious educators. Many parents are exhausted and feel they just don't have time for this, and so "keeping up with the Joneses" is killing our faith communities.

Collectivism shows up when we invest in our faith community, knowing that our needs will be met, our minds will be challenged, and our hearts will be opened. Collectivism shows up when we are given second and third chances, welcomed back a thousand times, because our covenant requires all of us to show one another this grace. Collectivism shows up when we deepen our understanding of ourselves by being in community with others, which is when our identity flows from the collective.

Bridging the ideals of collectivism and generosity, Bordas describes how relationships carry responsibility and refers to the Xhosa concept of *ubuntu*, which she translates as "I am because we are." "Like a tribal drumbeat, *ubuntu* resonates across African cultures and wraps people together — my humanity is tied to your humanity. It is not an ethereal spiritual concept of oneness but a real day-to-day obligation to be sharing, open, and welcoming toward others. Since *ubuntu* signifies that one's identity and well-being depend on other people, it underscores the collective and the tribe. The familiar saying 'It takes a village to raise a child' reflects this and emphasizes people's communal responsibility to all children."

In *Parenting Beyond Your Capacity*, Nieuwhof and Joiner describe a ritual of connection that Nieuwhof created for his son's thirteenth year that reflects *ubuntu*. He invited five trusted people to spend a day with his son over the course of the summer, each imparting one spiritual truth and a piece of good advice. At summer's end, Nieuwhof gathered the five mentors for dinner with his family, and each shared a story of overcoming a difficulty in their own life and described the gifts they witnessed in his son. Each offered a blessing and promised to be a continuing presence in his son's life. Nieuwhof knew the experience would be powerful for his son, but he was surprised by the tears of the mentors as they listened to each other's stories. They shared their sense of isolation and loneliness in the world and said they wished they had had such a set of mentors.

At Beacon UU Congregation in Summit, New Jersey, where I served with Rev. Emilie Boggis, we began exploring ways to offer families similar mentors, connecting them with long-time members who could help them build relationships, discover their passions, and learn how to use their talents to "build the Beacon," or serve the community. The proportion of visiting families who returned to become part of our community increased as a result of this initiative.

As I write this, we are struggling with the devastating COVID-19 pandemic. We have had to develop a collective mindset in unusual and unexpected ways. In order to protect the community, we must remain physically separated. Our lives depend on this collective effort. And although I have often blamed social media and the Internet for isolation, as a single extroverted person who has not experienced human touch in almost a month, I do not know what I would do without social media and Zoom.

A silver lining of the situation is that many of us now have more time to tend to our communities: making meals for others, sewing masks for medical workers, and being in touch with friends and family more regularly. This unique time has also offered parents opportunities to joyfully engage their children in our faith. I am now preparing Sunday morning sessions for whole families, not just children, to do at home. A parent recently wrote to me, "This was amazing! Thank you so much. We did it as a virtual session from our living room so both sets of grandparents could join." Another parent texted me pictures of her son and daughter, six and eight years old, creating a family Wonder Box, and added that it was the only time in days that they had played together peacefully. Colleagues have arranged for children and seniors in their faith communities to talk each week, for families to meet in neighborhood Zoom circles, and for congregants to host virtual open mics for all ages. We have all shifted to online worship, of course, and live chat has been a wonderful way for congregants to connect during the service and to share their joys and concerns.

It will be interesting to see how our congregations change as a result of this pandemic. But I know that our systems will always revert to preexisting power structures if we are not intentional about changing them. Intention requires us to regularly ask why we allow such structures to exist in our congregations. Although some age-segregated programming is needed, in the context of family ministry we must ask whether we should retain the structures that divide us by age. In the spirit of *Sankofa,* we must examine the past in order to create a better future.

Ultimately, when we commit to learning from multicultural, collectivist communities, we have the opportunity to help all families move from *I* to *we.* Parents can learn to parent from the perspective of relationship, as Joiner and Nieuwhof put it, instead of competence and abilities as our individualist culture would expect. Families of all kinds, with and without children, come to us looking for something different from what they are experiencing in our individualistic culture. They come looking to us for support. Can we give it to them? Can we be the antidote to this culture? Family ministry is how we all rise together.

How is your community the antidote to individualistic culture?

Creating Robust Communities of Care

Sky Gavis-Hughson

Do you see yourself as a giver or a recipient of care in your communities? What holds you back from receiving or offering care?

One Wednesday, after six months of being a part of the Community Care Team for my congregation, Sanctuary Boston, I logged on to my computer for Zoom worship. I had been on Zoom for most of the day already, I was emotionally drained from a morning migraine and a hard therapy session and what felt like an endless series of bad days, and I was really only there because I had committed to helping send real-time responses to the joys and sorrows that people would be sharing in the chat as one of the elements of our worship time.

Only I didn't actually send any comforting messages. Instead, I started sobbing partway through the service, turned off my camera, and curled into a ball on my bed with my computer propped on its side so I could still see what was happening. Instead of replying with words of support to others' joys and sorrows, I typed one of my own: *having a rough time with physical health that is starting to trickle into mental health.* Send. It felt like a major understatement, but it was what I could get out.

To my surprise, I received not one response but several. A friend texted to check in, someone I had sent a card to the week before wrote me an email wishing me healing, the other people working on the joys and sorrows response team with me asked what they could take off my plate. This warm, generous response of the congregation was, I imagine, in part a reflection of the time and effort I myself had poured into supporting people in the community. It was also part of a culture shift that the care team has been facilitating by modeling small ways of checking in, such as replying in chat to people's joys and sorrows. And, of course, I received support because I am surrounded by good people who care about me.

In showing up only to offer care to others, and in avoiding bringing my own sorrow to the space until I absolutely had to, I had forgotten something fundamental about the model of community care that I hold dear: to create communities of care, we must open ourselves to both giving and receiving care. In particular, I believe we are not fully allowing ourselves to be in community—to be seen, to be held, to be loved in community—if we see ourselves only as the givers of care, and never as the recipients. People's care is a mutual gift to both the giver and the recipient. We are offering someone the chance to see us, to experience the joy of loving someone well, to know the sense of belonging that comes from contributing to a community you yearn to belong to.

The Sanctuary care team was launched early in the pandemic, primarily as an emergency response team. Our work then was mostly outreach and connecting folks to resources. We offered money from our mutual aid fund, sent people cards and video messages of us singing, put together virtual check-in groups, and even delivered groceries to a congregant at high risk from COVID-19. As we've moved from acute crisis response to longer-term goals, the work of our team has shifted. Instead of hastily assembled check-in groups, we're working to build more robust systems of regular check-ins throughout our congregation. As I write this, we're coordinating socially distanced picnics, sending cards to people experiencing particularly high highs and low lows, and continuing to show up for people in the ways they ask us to. As circumstances shift and as we settle into whatever the long haul will look like, the work of our team will continue to evolve.

Still, I certainly never expected the team to be thriving six months into a pandemic. I kept expecting our work to become unsustainable. I've been in too many communities where everything we did together was happening from places of scarcity and exhaustion, and our work couldn't outlive the energy of a small core group. But on Sanctuary's care team, I've been surprised to find, our work has become more sustainable rather than less. There are many reasons for this, but here are a few that feel particularly salient:

1. We believe there should be no volunteering without joy. A core tenet of Sanctuary's model for leadership and community building is that if someone is volunteering, they are doing it because they want to, and not out of a sense of obligation or, worse, scarcity. When we ask people to do things, we seek an enthusiastic yes, not a begrudging or exhausted one.

2. We honor "no." Because most of us did not grow up in a culture of consent, we've been taught that saying "no" is rude, selfish, or downright wrong. When someone says "no" to something the care team asks of them, we

thank them for being honest with us and themselves
and for honoring their own capacity.

3. We remember that we are here to witness, not to fix
    or save each other. Many of us feel a deep need to "fix"
    hurt or dysfunction, or even to "save" those we see
    struggling. Recognizing the limits of what we can do,
    and the limits of what we *should* do, is necessary to
    doing care work and the work of community. Some-
    times, yes, we can fix problems—if someone has an
    unexpected bill one month, Sanctuary has a mutual
    aid fund we can offer them money from. We can never,
    however, "fix" people. Nor do we want to. What we can
    do is simply see people and welcome them exactly as
    they are.

4. We know that care comes in many forms. Nobody on
    our community care team is a minister or a therapist.
    We don't need to be. In our experience, offering peo-
    ple care isn't something you need to be trained for, it's
    something anyone can do. Don't get me wrong; therapy
    and other professional care are good and even neces-
    sary for a lot of people—I am one of those people—and
    can't be replaced by these kinds of amateur and lay
    care. But a text, a handwritten card, a voicemail sing-
    ing someone's favorite song—all of these are meaning-
    ful forms of care, and all of them build a community
    of care.

5. We believe that to be in community is to care and to
    be cared for. This is perhaps the difference between
    therapy and community. In therapy, we are offered

unconditional care, and we aren't asked to return the favor. That one-way flow of care is important and necessary to the work of therapy. In community, meanwhile, we are asked to care for each other and to accept, even if grudgingly, that we are cared for. The many-way flow of care is necessary to the work of community.

6. We trust that ministry by community members is not a sacrifice, it's a way of living our interdependence. We strongly believe that asking people to join in ministry work is a gift to them, not a burden on them. The task of ministry is not incumbent on any single person in the congregation; rather, our paid staff equip many of us for ministry, and coordinate and facilitate our work. To live into this principle is to live into our interdependence, our sacred responsibility to love and care for each other and to be loved and cared for in return.

The idea that community care is something that all of us in community are both asked to give and able to receive has reshaped my own vision of what it means to be in community. This care doesn't have to come in grand gestures or huge commitments of time, energy, or finances. Community asks us to bring whatever we have to offer. To bring it consistently, and joyfully, and with love for those to whom we offer it. The nature and size of our contribution are in many ways immaterial — sometimes it is financial, sometimes it's sending check-in texts and cards, sometimes it's the ability to find laughter just about anywhere, sometimes it's sharing our own story and our vulnerability. All of these offerings are valuable, and all are necessary.

These are lessons that I learn over and over as I seek out spaces of loving community. I have spent the past year living intentionally with a group of people who were all total strangers when we moved to Boston a year ago. It hasn't been easy—I never expected it to be. It is *hard* to invest in a group of people you don't know. It is *hard* to trust. When we ask for something, we open ourselves to being let down. And sometimes we are let down. If we're in communities of care, though, the rewards will far outweigh the disappointments.

Caring for others with vigor, and letting others care for us, is the lifeblood of intentional community, whether it's a housing community, a congregation, or any other group of people assembled in commitment and love. Community calls us to keep showing up, even when it's hard, when we're tired, when all we can do is say, *I'm hurting today. Today I have nothing to give.* Community calls us to give in abundance: to give of our time, of our presence, of our authenticity. Community calls us to receive in abundance, too.

Think about the ways your congregation is set up to meet the basic human need of care. Consider all your congregational structures and activities: leadership structure, worship, budgeting, and more. Does your congregation approach care with a mindset of scarcity or with one of abundance?

No One Is Outside the Circle of Love

Rev. Elizabeth Nguyen

How do you define your own circle of love?

The morning in 2018 that Dr. Christine Blasey Ford testified her truth—and thousands of us testified our truths to each other, to our families, to our own hearts—I was not planning on listening. This was the confirmation hearing on Brett Kavanaugh's nomination to the U.S. Supreme Court. I was in Minnesota for work and not feeling particularly grounded or hopeful.

I got into a Lyft to go to a meeting in a coffee shop, and the driver was listening to Dr. Blasey Ford testify.

For many of us there is nothing and everything to say about surviving harm and violence and then being reminded, again, in the strangest of places and in expected and unexpected moments, of what happened. A million layers of feeling and thought and pain and resilience recur again and again.

Hours later, I realized I had forgotten my laptop in the coffee shop.

One of the core questions of community and belonging is what we do when harm happens. How can we believe in belonging and the transformational power of connection when our communities are harmed? Earlier that morning I had heard the artist and organizer Ricardo Levins Morales

speak. In talking about the hearings, the Puerto Rican free-
dom struggle, and trying to love under an administration
committed to hate, he said, "Liberation struggles are about
restoring power to people whose power has been taken away.
Which is also a definition of trauma healing. Be a wetland.
Detoxify what is upstream. Pass on liberation."

I'm no ecologist, but I know what Ricardo meant: whatever goes into a wetland comes out less toxic, more healed,
less poisonous. I know that wetlands buffer plants and animals and ecosystems and people against the extremes of hur-
ricanes and floods and monsoons.

Be a wetland. Let whatever touches you or your communities be transformed to cause less harm, less harm, less harm.

Wetlands are organic and natural and fragile and fallible.
Strong and tenacious and also far too easy to uproot, pollute,
destroy.

None of us should ever receive pain or harm or violence.
We should not have to be wetlands. We should not have to
fight like hell to not pass it on.

And in the world we live in, we are hurt. We are in pain.
We survive violence.

Some cultures teach that when someone harms another
person, they don't belong anymore. They are no longer inside
the circle, no longer part of the community. Other cultures
teach that when someone harms, the circle changes. Boundaries have to be set to stop the harm. The person who harmed
has to choose to change their behavior and make right for
their wrong. They have to find their way back to themselves.
But they are never outside the circle of love. That circle holds
them. It is an invitation and an orientation, no matter how
unearned, that there is always a way toward love. Patriarchy

and white supremacy are rampaging through our world, killing and harming so many. Calling in, calling out, and cancel
culture can both save lives and hurt them, bring justice and
confuse it. My words here are written with humility about all
I do not know and therefore cannot say about all these truths
and all that I am learning, and they are grounded in the teaching that revelation is never sealed. These words are about
what I have learned about harm, belonging, and holding the
circle of love strong. Not because those who are destroying
our lives deserve to be excused or coddled, but because harm
is part of our lives and I want a way through that means that
I don't pass it on.

In a blog post entitled "Dr Ford's Dignity," the writer
and facilitator adrienne maree brown says, "we are survivors
who have learned and are learning to alchemize our pain
into futures that don't hurt our children's children. our stories are our slingshots, and we are moving forward. and none
of us move alone" (adriennemareebrown.net/2018/09/28/
dr-fords-dignity).

One way to explain transformative or restorative justice,
an approach to moving through harm that prioritizes accountability and healing instead of punishment, is by talking about
the way many of us intuitively respond to children. Suppose a
child steals their friend's toy. Or hits their parent. Or says, "I
hate you" to their sibling. At our best, human selves, we know
that to move forward is not to banish the child, not to cast
them out of the circle of love. Not to hit them back or say, "I
hate you, too." It's to stop the pain they caused. To figure out
what would make it better or more right. Give the toy back.
Apologize. Share something they appreciate about their sibling. Learn how to breathe. Or yell. Or hit a pillow instead.

These responses remind us that transformative and restorative justice are not new, jargony, social justice things. They're
skills and ways of being that we have probably experienced
in our own lives, regardless of what words we used for them.

Some of us, and some of our families, have been so con-
torted and harmed by systems of poverty, patriarchy, white
supremacy that we don't respond to challenges from our best
selves. Some of us have had to leave families or set good,
holy boundaries with them in order to heal that harm. But
for many of us, our experiences of family by choice, by origin,
or by community, can serve as powerful reminders that we
can deal, and have dealt, with conflict, harm, and accountability in ways that do not involve passing on that harm to
others. That create clear boundaries to prevent further harm
and that also do not dispose of people or deny them their
humanity.

Dejuan was nine years old when Hurricane Katrina hit
New Orleans. He never had problems in school prior to the
storm, but his family had to leave the Ninth Ward and stay
with relatives in Texas. He said in an interview, "I was really
scared. We had to leave everything behind. We had nowhere
to stay. Shelters. Being around people we didn't know. I
remember being in a dark place, being lost," he said. "I think
about Katrina all the time."

One morning in New Orleans I woke up at the end of a
work conference to the news that two of my coworkers at the
Unitarian Universalist Association had been hurt, very badly,
in a robbery. And twenty-two-year-old Dejuan was one of the
people who did it.

adrienne maree brown has said, "Trauma makes weap-
ons of us all" (interview by Justin Scott Campbell, medium

.com/@jscottcampbell/trauma-makes-weapons-of-us-
all-an-interview-with-adrienne-maree-brown-e6ef7453fd28).

I have seen how wars of many kinds can make anyone
a killer and anyone a survivor. How they make many people both. How punishing the people who hurt me did not
change them. Over the years I've participated in many efforts
at transformative justice that have tried to center healing and
nonpunitive accountability and to transform the contexts that
lead to harm. There have been pain and grief, beauty and con-
fusion, hopelessness and power. More than anything, these
efforts have felt like the deepest growing edge of my spirituality: my efforts to grapple with my own ability to harm
others. To survive harm. To be the wetland that I—and all of
us—should.never have to be.

Mariame Kaba, a visionary prison-abolitionist organizer,
says in an interview by Sarah Jaffe, "We have to make violence unthinkable in our culture. . . . We have to be mindful
of the fact that the very thing we say we want to end—violence—is being perpetrated by that very same system. We are
trying to end violence with more violence" ("From 'Me Too'
to 'All of Us,'" inthesetimes.com/article/incarceration-sexual-
assualt-me-too-rape-culture-organizing-resistance).

Many days after that morning in New Orleans, as my
coworkers and their loved ones sat in hospitals together
praying and hoping and trying to understand everything
that could not be undone, horrific videos of the violence
played nonstop on TV from Louisiana to Massachusetts. We
began to talk about whether there was a different way forward. About whether in this most charged context—a racist
New Orleans tourism bureau and a racist mayor and a racist
chief of police and four young Black men and two white

tourists — there was any way to be a wetland. To alchemize the horror.

I don't really have words to express the heartache and love and risk that went into trying to do that. The introduction of these ideas of transformative justice in the middle of crisis. The incredible New Orleans leaders who went to every court date, who raised money for commissary, who talked with the families of the young men and the staff of Covenant House, the shelter where they had been living. Janet Connors, a Boston elder and restorative justice circle holder, taught us that punishment comes down from above and accountability rises up from within. She led my coworkers in a circle process to share their feelings and find next steps.

In the end we did not keep them out of prison, though both of my coworkers wrote letters to the court asking for that, and both letters were read and entered into the record by the judge and the prosecutor. In the end, Dejuan, Joshua, Rashaad, Nicholas are serving unimaginable time. In the end, my coworkers are still and will always be healing from violence that cannot be undone. In the end, Dejuan, Joshua, Rashaad, Nicholas are still and will always be healing from violence that cannot be undone.

In an interview, my coworker Tim talked about why he asked for no prison time. He said he did so "not because he is more compassionate than others or that he personally likes the people who attacked him. He simply believes that if the end goal is creating a safer society, the means to achieving that can't be locking everyone up." He said, "Anything left untreated is a thing that's going to come back and cause some damage to somebody. . . . And, in this instance, it caused a lot of damage to me." Only healing heals. Kicking people out of the circle of community, whether through poverty or climate chaos or incarceration, only passes on the harm.

In the end, prosecutors, city officials, congregants, residents of New Orleans and of Boston did have a glimpse of a different approach. A glimpse of an approach that says, "Not on my behalf will you deny my siblings their humanity." That says that even on our worst days we can know another world is coming. Even if we will not fully know it in this lifetime, another way is coming. A way that does not put anyone outside of the circle, a way that passes on liberation and alchemizes pain.

The end has not yet come, for this story at least. Many of the folks who have been touched by it are now involved in transformative and restorative justice work.

In her restorative and transformative circles, Janet often tells her own story: the story of the murder of her son. Of her pain and heartache as the case moved through the criminal justice system. Of the healing she thought would come from the punishment of the guilty. Of the healing that never did come from that—but did come, in some new, tender, raw way, from the dialogue she was able to have with those who so harmed her and her family. It's not an accident many call her Mama J. She lost her son and gained so many of us as children in this work.

May we be the ones who do not pass on pain.

It should not be our job. We should live in a world where none of us is ever harmed. And yet this is our world. May we lead ourselves into more wellness, more love, less harm. May we be wetlands.

How does harm get passed on through your community?

We Hold Hope Close

Rev. Theresa I. Soto

In this community, we hold hope close. We don't always know what comes next, but that cannot dissuade us. We don't always know just what to do, but that will not mean that we are lost in the wilderness. We rely on the certainty beneath, the foundation of our values and ethics. We are the people who hold to love as our guiding star and to the truth that we are greater together than we are alone. Our hope does not live in some glimmering, indistinct future. Rather, we know the way to the world of which we dream, and we know that by covenant and movement forward, by taking one right action and the next, one day we will arrive at home.

Resources

Class Action: The Struggle with Class in Unitarian Universalism, Commission on Appraisal, 2017.

Dismantling Racism, Kenneth Jones and Tema Okun, dismantlingracism.org.

Elite: Uncovering Classism in Unitarian Universalist History, Mark W. Harris, 2010.

"Embracing Social Class Inclusion: A Worship Service," UU Class Conversations, uuclassconversations.org/wp-content/uploads /Embracing-Social-Class-Inclusion-Worship-Resources.pdf.

"Family Ministry at UUCB: The Birth of the Binghamton Model," Ann Kadlecek, uua.org/files/pdf/f/family_min_binghamton _kadlecek.pdf.

"Five Practices of Welcome Renewal," UUA, uua.org/lgbtq /welcoming/program/five-practices-welcome-renewal.

Organizing: People, Power, Change. Marshall Ganz. commonslibrary .org/organizing-people-power-change, 2014.

Salsa, Soul, and Spirit: Leadership for a Multicultural Age, Second Edition, Juana Bordas, 2012.

"Supporting Trans/Non-Binary Youth in Your Congregation," UUA, uua.org/youth/identity-formation/resources/trans-non -binary-youth.

"Transgender 101: Identity, Inclusion, and Resources," UUA, uua.org/lgbtq/identity/transgender.

"Transgender Inclusion & Affirmation: Questions to Consider," UUA LGBTQ Ministries Office, uua.org/files/documents/lgbtq /trans_inclusion_qs.pdf.

Organizations

The **Faith Matters Network** (faithmattersnetwork.org) "catalyzes
personal and social change by equipping community organizers, faith leaders, and activists with resources for connection,
spiritual sustainability, and accompaniment."

The Sanctuary Boston (thesanctuaryboston.org) is "a community of vibrant worship and real connection. . . . At the Sanctuary Boston, we believe that everyone deserves to experience
beloved community. We are a community grounded in Unitarian Universalism and open to seekers of all kinds."

Solidarity Is: The Building Movement Project (buildingmovement
.org) "supports and pushes the nonprofit sector to tackle
the most significant social issues of our times by developing
research, creating tools and training materials, providing guid-
ance, and facilitating networks for social change."

The **Transforming Hearts Collective** (transformingheartscollective
.org) "represents a vision of a world in which queer and trans
people can show up fully as ourselves in all of the places we call
home. We support spaces for LGBTQ people to access resilience, healing, and spirituality, and we resource faith communities and other groups for the work of radical inclusion and
culture shift."

UU Wellspring: Spiritual Deepening for the UU Soul
(uuwellspring.org) "is a 10-month spiritual deepening course
for Unitarian Universalists. Group members experience deep
listening and spiritual reflection in small groups of about ten,
inspiring personal and community transformation."

Community of Contributors

Editor **Linnea Nelson** (she/her) is a certified spiritual director companioning adults, youth, and children on their spiritual journeys. She served as president of the Liberal Religious Educators Association (LREDA) and is the executive director of UU Wellspring, a yearlong spiritual deepening program for Unitarian Universalists. She is credentialed by the UUA at the highest level for religious educators. Community has been a lifelong focus for Linnea, and she believes that religious community is the place to bring our whole selves to enrich and empower the greater good. Linnea and her husband, Ted, are active members of First Unitarian Church of Orlando, Florida.

Rev. Summer Albayati (she/her) is a UU Muslim of Iraqi descent who serves as congregational life staff in the Pacific Western Region of the Unitarian Universalist Association. Rev. Albayati has been playing the Arabic drum professionally since the age of twelve, and has shared her gifts in worship, concerts, and social justice venues most of her life. These experiences gave her a foundation from which to explore the intersections of speaking prophetically, making music, healing spirits, and doing social justice work, all while reflecting on Islam as a theology of liberation.

Laura Beth Brown (she/her) has been a religious educator for twenty years, primarily in the metro New York area, where she has served five congregations. She is now the director of lifespan religious education at the Unitarian Universalist Congregation of Atlanta. A proud member of the Liberal Religious Educators Association (LREDA), Laura Beth was a LREDA good officer for six years, served as president of the Metro New York chapter, and is now a UUA-certified interim religious educator. She also created the online volunteer strategy course Stop Recruiting Start Retaining for the UU Leadership Institute, led Embracing Family Ministry workshops at national conferences of both LREDA and the Unitarian Universalist Ministers Association (UUMA), and consults with congregations in areas of governance, family ministry, and volunteer strategy.

Sky Gavis-Hughson (they/them) is a community care builder and jigsaw puzzle lover. They are a first-year MSW student at Simmons, where they hope to learn about equipping others with the tools to build meaningful lives and create thriving communities. Sky is a spiritual Jewish UU-curious community member of Sanctuary Boston, where they have served on the Board, the Community Care Team, and as a small group facilitator. Sky lives in Boston and enjoys riding their bike, crocheting, and cooking for their housemates and friends.

Aisha K. Hauser (she/her), Master of Social Work, has been a religious educator since 2003 and has served three congregations. She was also the director of children and family programs at the UUA. Aisha received the 2018 Angus H. MacLean Award for Excellence in Religious Education. In

2017 Aisha cofounded the UU White Supremacy Teach-In (uuteachin.org), with Christina Rivera and Kenny Wiley. This included creating teach-in materials to support Unitarian Universalist congregations in understanding and fighting against white supremacy. Aisha is a contributor to the groundbreaking 2017 collection *Centering: Navigating Race, Authenticity, and Power in Ministry*, edited by Mitra Rahnema, and cowrote, with Gail Forsyth-Vail, the accompanying study guide. She is the president of the Liberal Religious Educators Association (LREDA) and on the Lead Ministry Team of the Church of the Larger Fellowship.

Julica Hermann de la Fuente (she/her) is the director of liberation and transformation ministries at the First Universalist Church of Minneapolis and is completing her journey to ministerial ordination. Born and raised in Mexico City, she became committed to social justice when she attended college in the United States and has been an antiracism and antioppression educator and trainer for over two decades. Her fancy diplomas and titles include a master's degree from Meadville Lombard Theological School, an MSW (and almost a PhD!) from the University of Michigan, and several certifications in life coaching. When not on shift for the resistance, Julica can be found playing with fabric; making costumes for her children, Aliana and Skyler; looking for excuses to frost fancy cakes; and reading optimistic sci-fi and fantasy possibilities of a just and equitable universe.

Nichole Hodges-Abbasi (she/her) is the director of religious education at the Unitarian Universalist Congregation of Frederick, Maryland. She is also a music teacher and labor rights activist and is passionate about creating meaningful connections with others. Her children are Zachi Abbasi (he/him) and Tobi Abbasi (he/him). Zachi is ten years old and enjoys reading, playing outside on his scooter, traveling, and video games. He has a terrific sense of humor and hopes to travel the world. Tobi is nine years old. He loves to jump on his trampoline and play with his Beyblades and also enjoys anime and playing with his friends. Tobi hopes to write his own book series, to be entitled The Life of an Anime Kid.

Dr. Janice Marie Johnson (she/her) is a mother, grandmother, aunt, sibling, friend, and colleague who treasures her unique relationships as she strives to live into her maxim, *Masakhane*, a rich and resonant word from the Nguni family of languages of South Africa, which includes Zulu and Xhosa. Loosely translated into English, it means, "Let us build together." Dr. Johnson is co-director of ministries and faith development at the UUA. Committed to making multiculturalism real, Janice is a Jamaican, a New Yorker, an internationalist, and a "third-culture kid" who grew up all over the world and has also worked with Unitarian Universalist congregations worldwide. As an educator, she previously served as director of lifespan religious education at the Community Church of New York.

L. C. Magee (they/them) is a former youth leader in Unitarian Universalism, a current student at the University of Mary Washington, and an avid fiction and nonfiction writer. In their free time they enjoy working with clubs on campus, loudly discussing fantasy novels, keeping up with friends, and generally questioning everything around them in the spirit of the interconnected web of existence.

Rev. Manish Mishra-Marzetti (he/him) serves as senior minister of the First Unitarian Universalist Congregation of Ann Arbor, Michigan. He has served extensively in UU leadership, including as president of the Diverse and Revolutionary Unitarian Universalist Multicultural Ministries (DRUUMM), as a member of the UUA Board of Trustees, and as a member of the UUSC Board. Prior to entering the ministry, he was a U.S. diplomat during the Clinton administration. He loves desert hiking and his amazing kids and husband.

Denise Moorehead (they/them) is a marketing, communications, and training strategist who has worked with organizations committed to promoting the common good, including the Unitarian Universalist Service Committee. Committed to building community across differences, Denise founded UU Class Conversations with the late Rev. Dr. Dorothy Emerson. Denise is also a a graduate and former board member of Leadership MetroWest. They are a member of First Parish Framingham, the fiscal sponsor of UU Class Conversations.

Kristin C. Moyer (she/her) is a graduate of Beloit College with a degree in theatre and English composition. She is a poet, storyteller, visual arts designer, and blogger (Diary of Not a Wimpy Widow, notawimpywidow.com). Kristin is a member of the Unitarian Universalist Congregation of Fairfax, Virginia.

Rev. Elizabeth Nguyen (she/her) is a Midwesterner at heart, lives in Boston, and is learning all the time about liberation, solidarity, courage, and cowardice. She is the immigration bond coordinator with the National Bail Fund Network and previously did faith-based justice work and youth organizing.

She is passionate about progressive organizing in the Vietnamese American community, building power across prison walls, and feeding people.

Christina Rivera (she/her) is a religious educator and co-lead minister of the Church of the Larger Fellowship. She was the first Latina and the first religious educator elected to the UUA Board of Trustees and served the UUA not only as a trustee but also as secretary and financial secretary. In 2017 Chris cofounded the UU White Supremacy Teach-In (uuteachin .org). In 2018 she founded Called to Justice, a faith-based consulting group focused on impactful leadership and congregational development for Unitarian Universalists committed to justice ministries. She has the faith and support of her husband, Chris, and twin sons, Andreas and Miguel, who, along with her ancestors, form the foundation for her calling to Unitarian Universalist ministry.

Julie Romero (she/her) has been associated with Unitarian Universalism since she was a young child; one of her first memories is of the basement of Boston's Arlington Street Church. She has been a member of youth groups (including Liberal Religious Youth), a congregation member, a church school teacher, a religious education coordinator, and a volunteer at Star Island. The connections she has made continue to influence her life. Julie lives in Rhode Island with her husband and one of her sons.

Rev. Mykal O'Neal Slack (he/him) is the community minister for worship and spiritual care for Black Lives of Unitarian Universalism (BLUU), an organization and a growing spiritual community that provides support, resources, and care for Black UUs across the diaspora. He is also one of the cofounders of the Transforming Hearts Collective, an organizing ministry that helps to both cocreate spaces of healing and spiritual resiliency for queer, trans, and nonbinary folks and to provide congregations with resources for the work of radical welcome and culture shift.

Rev. Theresa I. Soto (they/them) is the senior minister of the First Unitarian Church of Oakland, California, and the author of *Spilling the Light: Meditations on Hope and Resilience* (Skinner House, 2019). They have enjoyed interim ministry and chaplaincy with veterans. They live in Ashland, Oregon, with their partner, Rev. Sean Parker Dennison, and have served as a community minister with the Rogue Valley Unitarian Universalist Fellowship in Ashland, Oregon.

Rev. Leslie Takahashi is the former chair of the Commission on Institutional Change, which was established by the UUA Board of Trustees to analyze structural racism and white supremacy culture within the UUA. She is the co-author, with Chip Roush and Leon Spencer, of *The Arc of The Universe is Long: Anti-racism and the Unitarian Universalist Association* (Skinner House 2008) and a contributor to a number of professional publications and meditation collections. Finding Unitarian Universalism in her twenties, she has served extensively at the congregational, District and national levels both within the Unitarian Universalist Association and the UU Ministers Association. Her current passion is the day-to-day work of building beloved community at the Mt. Diablo Unitarian Universalist Church, where she serves as lead minister. Her greatest accountability is to her children and grandchild.

Dr. Jenice L. View (she/her) is an associate professor Emerita at George Mason University and a member of the Board of Trustees of Meadville Lombard Theological School, where she also serves as an adjunct professor and retreat leader for the Beloved Conversations Meditations on Race and Ethnicity workshops. She is the creator and host of *Urban Education: Issues and Solutions,* an award-winning GMU-TV cable television program. She is coeditor of *Why Public Schools? Voices from the United States and Canada* (Information Age, 2013) and the award-winning *Putting the Movement Back into Civil Rights Teaching: A Resource Guide for Classrooms and Communities* (Teaching for Change and the Poverty and Race Research Action Council, 2004), and *Antiracist Professional Development for In-Service Teachers* (IGI Global, 2020). She is also the coauthor of "We Who Defy Hate: An Interfaith Preparation for Social Justice," a curriculum designed to accompany the 2016 PBS documentary *Defying the Nazis: The Sharps' War.* She holds degrees from Syracuse University, Princeton University, and the Union Institute and University.

Laura Weiss (she/her) is worship director and director of music and arts at the Unitarian Universalist Congregation of Fairfax, Virginia, having joined the congregation in 2016. She has also served as music director or conductor for artistic organizations throughout the United States and has served various faith communities for more than twenty years. Laura grew up near Baltimore but spent seventeen years in New England before returning to the DC metro region. She holds a bachelor's in music and a master's in education from the Center for Creative Teaching at Bennington College in Vermont and is an Orff- and Kodaly-trained educator who has taught in numerous educational settings. Laura is passionate about music and ministry. She believes that music in worship should be relevant and intimately performed and that it is through the arts that the deepest parts of our emotional and shared experiences can be felt. Laura, her husband, Josiah, and their daughter, Adia, live in Vienna, Virginia.